A Ranger's Pocket Guide to Yellowstone National Park

Simple, Concise Ranger Day Plans We Share with Visitors Every Day

R.D. Nullmeyer

DEDICATION

I'd like to dedicate this book to every ranger in every park in the entire National Park Service system. These are the few that work tirelessly educating, protecting, and helping visitors get the most from a visit to a national park. They also work diligently maintaining and managing all the special places we call national parks. Without their endless energy and devotion to going the extra mile trying to help every park visitor have the best experience they can, wherever they may be, all of us would lose the opportunity to experience some very special places. As well, these special places wouldn't exist if they weren't set aside for all to share and enjoy, now and in the future.

Thank you fellow rangers.

CONTENTS

INTRODUCTION

As a seasonal park ranger working for the National Park Service, a division of the Department of the Interior, we're asked all kinds of questions about Yellowstone National Park. It's our mission to help each visitor maximize their stay and experience as much of the park as possible as long as we keep them safe while doing so. Along the way, we're asked tons of questions about the park. They range from "How close can I get to a bison?" to "How can I see the entire park in two days?" You name it, we've probably been asked the question.

Some of these questions can be pretty outlandish. This reminds me of the guy who made a comment to me at the end of the National Park's Centennial season that it would "be better to try and teach the animals to stay away from the people instead of trying to teach the people to stay away from the animals." He finished his suggestion saying he was just trying to make a point. And he DID! So let's look at the merits of his proposal. IF we were able to train the animals to stay away from the visitors, then we'd only have to train the newborns each subsequent year. That would make it much less labor-intensive to train the rookie animals thereafter. Trying to 'train' the visitors is a never-ending project in frustration, because the visitor mix is constantly changing. Every year we get millions of visitors to the park and that visitor mix changes each season as well. That would lend some credence to training the animals which is now starting to look like a more viable alternative. Not!

But let's take this one step further. Can you imagine if the park service spent the time and money to train thousands and thousands of animals to stay safe distances from people, and the training actually worked? That assumes the animals are intelligent enough to absorb the training, right? OK. So if the animals CAN absorb the training, then doesn't that imply that the humans who can't actually follow the safe distance from animals requirements, are now dumber than the animals? What's wrong with that picture? Lots!! The guy has a point though!

I work the summer season at Yellowstone National Park at a visitor's center desk. Besides answering questions about the park, I also present many interpretive programs to the general public as part of my duties, as most interpretive rangers do. We also sell an assortment of passes, permits, and licenses, as well as give short talks about various aspects of the park including safety talks. Actually, the vast majority of questions we're asked are normal, simple, very reasonable questions like, "Where's the nearest bathroom?" Or, "Which way do I go to get to (wherever) in the park?" Or, "How many miles of trails in the park?" etc. You get the idea. The job is very rewarding for me as I truly enjoy helping people have a nice vacation at a place that is about as awe-inspiring as nature can get. Yellowstone National Park is a pretty special place!

As seasonal rangers we come from all sorts of

backgrounds and life experiences. Some of my fellow rangers have backgrounds in teaching, nursing, insurance, engineering, and one was an arthroscopic surgeon. I myself come from a background in real estate. Because seasonal rangers come from such dissimilar backgrounds, it gives us the advantage of being able to assist park visitors with their planning and enjoyment of the park. You see, we pay attention to how our fellow rangers are answering questions because of their previous life experiences. We then use that to modify how we share the park with the people we talk to. Different people from dissimilar backgrounds have different perceptions, and we use that trick to our betterment so each visitor can have the best park experience.

There are also various types of rangers in most national parks, Yellowstone included. There are interpretation rangers who assist visitors with information about the park, what's available for them to see and experience, as well as protecting and supervising outdoor areas while verifying that visitors are complying with park rules and regulations. I am an interpretation ranger. There are also law enforcement rangers who essentially do the important job of keeping the park safe, much as police and sheriff deputies do back home. There are maintenance rangers who help keep the park in the best shape possible given the funds available for them to do so. We have rangers who do naturalist work, and rangers that are specialists in forestry, botany, zoology, geology and biology, as well as administrative, management and supervisory rangers.

The park is quite different from most other national parks in one very important way. Most other national parks have one or two things that set them apart from other parks, like some historical significance as at Gettysburg, or maybe a distinctive feature like the Everglades, or maybe even patriotic importance like the Statue of Liberty. Yellowstone National Park – our country's first national park – has multiple unique features all wrapped into one. We have over ten thousand hydro-thermal and geo-thermal features in the park primarily because of the volcano. Yes, the park sits on top of one of the world's largest, active super-volcanos. We also have large quantities of wild animals like bison, elk, grizzly bears, black bears, and wolves. We have flora and fauna all over the place. We have raptors and wild birds. We have an array of fish. We have huge expanses of trees, as well as an enormous range of other plants and animals. And, oh, did I mention the park is just under 3,500 square miles [9,065 square kilometers] in size, has over a thousand miles [1,609 kilometers] of trails, has almost three hundred waterfalls, and occupies a large chunk of the northwest corner of the State of Wyoming? Maybe all of this is how some really out-of-control misconceptions that visitors have about the park are incubated. I'm not really sure where these thoughts come from, which increases the challenge for us as rangers to help visitors have a safe and enjoyable visit.

Now I also want to be sure that anyone reading this book understands that the vast majority of people visiting the park, that I've come in contact with anyway, are very normal and well-intentioned people. They're just in the park to have a good time on vacation and see as much as they can. None of these visitors would ever even think about some of the questions I've dealt with in past seasons. But as we all know, there are always a few in the crowd who have different ideas about things. It's these people who ask the senseless questions, and it's these people who need the extra attention to straighten out their misconceptions. This is one of the challenges of being a ranger. Our ranger hearts are totally pointed at one goal, and one goal only. That is, hoping that each visitor has an enjoyable, educational and safe vacation in the park, despite any previous misconceptions.

So thanks to the thousands of visitors who had questions about the park. It's those questions that gave me the idea to create the Ranger Day Plans included in this book.

I hope you enjoy reading a little about how you can plan your own visit to Yellowstone National Park and see the most in whatever time you can set aside. I also hope you have an enjoyable and, hopefully, safe visit to Yellowstone National Park with some guidance, practicality and caution from at least this one ranger.

Chapter One

A Little Bit about Yellowstone National Park

People come to Yellowstone National Park with all sorts of misconceptions. So I thought I'd take a few minutes and try and explain some of the facts about the park to help you be a bit more informed.

The park was founded as our country's first national park when Congress sent a bill to the then President of the United States, Ulysses S. Grant (of Civil War fame), who signed it into law on March 1, 1872. Soon after that the United States Army Cavalry occupied the park as its first managers. The U.S. Army Cavalry was there until 1918. Two years earlier, in 1916, the National Park Service was formed, also by an act of Congress, to manage the nation's growing list of parks. During those two initial years, 1916 through 1918, both federal agencies – the U.S. Army Cavalry and the National Park Service – managed the park. Now we all know today how well having two federal agencies managing the same thing at the same time might go, ha? So it's pretty easy to conclude that it probably didn't work out too well for either federal agency way back then either. Finally in 1918, the U.S. Army Cavalry passed on management of Yellowstone to the National Park Service and the Cavalry left the park for the last time. The National Park Service has managed Yellowstone National Park, and the rest of our nation's parks, ever since.

Yellowstone National Park is just under 3,500 square

miles [9,065 square kilometers] in size, which equates to about 2.2 million acres. That's a VERY big park. The main roads in the park are called the Grand Loop which consists of the Upper Grand Loop Road and the Lower Grand Loop Road. Together, the two loop roads form a figure eight. The Upper Grand Loop Road takes about three and a half hours to circumnavigate without stopping, while the Lower Grand Loop Road takes about four or more hours to get all the way around, also without stopping. That means no bathroom breaks, no stopping to eat, not fair stopping for gas, and you certainly can't stop to view any animals, waterfalls, or features in the park. It's just the driving time based upon the parks maximum speed limit of 45 miles per hour [72 KPH], or less if posted. There are five entry gates: one in the west entering from the town of West Yellowstone, Montana; one in the northwest corner of the park at Mammoth near the town of Gardiner, Montana; one at the northeast corner of the park near the towns of Cooke City and Silvergate, Montana; one on the east side of the park that has the city of Cody, Wyoming about 55 miles [89 kilometers] to the east of it; and finally the south gate that intersects the Rockefeller Parkway and access to Grand Teton National Park (also in Wyoming) near Jackson, Wyoming.

Yellowstone National Park has over 1,000 miles [1,609 kilometers] of hiking trails, 67 species of mammals, 285 classes of birds, 16 types of fish, 9 species of conifer trees, over 1,000 kinds of native flowers, over 10,000 hydro-thermal and geo-thermal features, a super-volcanic caldera that measures about 45 miles [72 kilometers] west to east by 30 miles [48 kilometers] north to south, about 900 historic buildings, more than 1,800 archeological sites, 26 associated Native American tribes, the largest lake in North America (over 7,000 feet [2,134 meters] in elevation making it an alpine lake), 290 waterfalls (and counting), 5 park entrances, 466 miles [750 kilometers] of roads, more than 15 miles [24 kilometers] of boardwalks, and 9 visitor's centers and museums. It takes almost three hours to drive from the west side to the east side of the park. We also have large numbers of grizzly bears, black bears, bison, elk, and wolves plus large populations of other critters as well – and they are ALL WILD. About eighty percent of the trees in the park are Lodge Pole Pines, mostly in the southern portion of the park, with the remaining trees a mixture of White Bark Pine, Aspen, conifers and others, mostly located in the northern portion of the park.

One of the main features in the park is the volcano related feature called geysers. Old Faithful is one of them. To help you understand more fully how a geyser works, picture Old Faithful erupting in your mind, and I'll explain how that eruption happens. Think about a teapot. That's right, an average, ordinary, everyday teapot. Fill it with water and place it on the stove. It takes a while, but eventually the water boils. Pour out, say, one cup of hot water and fill the teapot with water again. It doesn't take much time at all for the teapot to boil again, right? Sure. But if you had poured out, say, four cups of hot water and refilled it, it would take a LOT more time for it to boil again. So, each time Old Faithful Geyser erupts, the Park Service measures how high and for how long the eruption lasts. The higher and longer the eruption, the more water is used up just like the teapot. So the next eruption will take a little longer before it happens. Because of this completely natural occurrence, we are unable to predict further than the very next eruption of the geyser. This is why when visitors ask rangers for a "geyser schedule," we can't accommodate them, because there is no schedule. We never know how large or small the next eruption will be. So each eruption, predicts the next eruption. This is also why you see an eruption time and then plus or minus ten minutes (for Old Faithful anyway) for the eruption times we post to the public.

Our visitation in 2014 was 3.2 million visitors in a summer season lasting around five months and has increased about 300,000 visitors each year. 2016 (the National Park's Centennial year) the visitation was about 4.2 million and future visitation is expected to meet or exceed those same marks and increase dramatically. Simply put ... the parks visitor load is immense.

We have visitors from just about every country in the world that visit Yellowstone each season. Most are very nice people who have one thing on their mind – having a good time while respecting the cultural and natural beauty of Yellowstone and leaving it in better condition than when they arrived. And as rangers, we

LOVE that attitude. BUT, we also have people who come here thinking this is their place alone and everyone else should get out of their way. These people are the challenges, and it's these people that helped to inspire this book. I thank them for being a challenge because without them the truly misguided and under-thought-out questions would not have to be answered, and this book wouldn't exist. So thank you challenging people. Thank You.

I'd also like to take a moment and thank those visitors who come fairly well prepared, who took the time to plan a little about what they can see in the park, and know what they will not have time to experience. Most visitors, surprisingly, do not plan at all – and this is sad. These visitors often fly thousands and thousands of miles to get here, go through the process of renting a car, then may drive for up to five hours (sometimes more) to get to the park, and have no idea of where to go or what they can see. No planning whatsoever. What did they do on that 15 hour plane ride to get to the park in the first place? Maybe they could have done a little research and some planning? Maybe read a little about where they're going? What a concept! The sad part is that 'not planning' seems to be the norm. Then these same visitors arrive, and they want to see the whole park, not miss anything, and they only have two days (because they didn't plan and don't realize how BIG the park is). They're astonished when we have to tell them that it's not going to happen. The park is just TOO BIG, things are very far apart, and they're not going to have the time to see all of it. You should see the dumbfounded looks we get.

So if nothing else comes out of this book, I hope and pray at least some of you who read this book take a few minutes and plan out what means the most for you to see. Please allow three or four days MINIMUM to visit the park. We love it when people approach the visitor center desk with a list of things they want to see in their hand, and they have the time set aside to actually see all of it. We grab a park map and ask them to tell us what they have on their list. We mark the map and explain things to them as they go. Because they've done the research, they understand most of what we're telling them, and we straighten them out on a few things they may have missed. It's actually a lot of fun for us. It really makes our day knowing that they cared enough to read a little about the park and write down what they wanted to see. Yellowstone National Park is truly a super-natural place, and all that much more magical if the visitors have some concept of what they want to see and have the time to see it. Now we'll always fill in the gaps when they forget to mention a really cool part of the park (Cool, by the way, is just an adjective I used here as most parts of the park are NOT cool at all, they're HOT!). And we're glad to do it. We really want every visitor to have a great experience. That's what being a ranger IS all about. Right?

OK. So here we go with the first step in your visit to the park. Pre-planning your visit is the next chapter. Keep reading.

Chapter Two

Pre-Planning Your Visit

So how do these Ranger Day Plans work?

The plans are derived from years of experience and are designed for easy use. They're arranged by how much time you have in the park. My best ranger advice is to start your pre-visitation plan months and months before your actual visit. Sit down and think about how much time you can devote to a visit to the park, then commit to that goal. Simply put, the park is huge. It takes lots of time to get around and see things because they're so spread out. As an example, it takes about four hours to drive from the north gate to the south gate of the park. It's a BIG place. My point is, you can't see all the best features if you only allow yourself a day or two. You'll be rushing all over the place and not have an enjoyable visit. People do this to themselves all the time, and I'd bet that when they leave the park they wish they'd managed their visit differently. So don't do that to yourself, OK?

With the concept in mind of how large the park is, the next pre-planning step is to attack your visit in a logical manner to maximize what you can see and minimize useless stops. So focus on which aspects of the park you'd like to see the most. Is it the geysers and thermal features like Old Faithful, Grand Prismatic Spring, and Mud Volcano? Is it seeing lots of wildlife like bison, elk, grizzly and black bears, and wolves? Maybe it's seeing loads of waterfalls? Perhaps you're into hiking, and that's what you'd like to do. What is it that you want to see and experience?

Also keep in mind that the animals go through life changes during the summer. For example, if it's grizzly bears you're most intrigued with – from a distance of course – come to the park early in the season, late May or early June. The grizzly bears have been out of hibernation for a few months but aren't used to seeing large numbers of people yet, so it's easier to see them.

If it's the bison or elk ruts you're after (the word "rut" is ranger talk for the mating season), you'll have to wait until mid-August for the bison rut and mid-September for the elk rut. The male bison display very aggressive behavior and fight for the right to 'be' with the females during their rut. So there's a bunch of head smashing, charging each other, and general 'posturing' going on. Pretty interesting. On the other hand during mid-September the male elk also charge each other and display aggressive behavior as bison do, but have one thing going for them that the bison don't. The male elk "bugle" (kind of like a weird scream) when collecting females for their harem of potential mates. The bugling is a challenge to other male elk to "just try and take them away from me."

So if one of those things are more interesting to you, then plan accordingly.

The last step in your pre-planning visitation plan is to merely merge how much time you've set aside to visit

Yellowstone National Park ... with what you want to see. So let me walk you through an example of planning your trip using the ranger pre-planning guidelines in this book. Let's say you have two days to visit the park. Look in the Table of Contents and migrate to the chapter where the Two Day Ranger Plan starts – Chapter Seven on page 61. On a Two Day Ranger Plan you'd be able to see some geysers, hot springs, bubbling mud, a BIG waterfall or two, and some wild animals. This is somewhat of a good sampling of what the park has to offer visitors.

The next stage of your planning would be to get a map of the park. If you have internet access you can go to

https://www.nps.gov/yell/planyourvisit/upload/YEL L_Tear-Off_Map2016.pdf

or type 'Yellowstone National Park Map' into your browser search box. Either way, you'll get the map of the park. If you'd rather have a full blown, official park map, you can write to the park at Visitor Services Office, Yellowstone National Park, P.O. Box 168, Yellowstone National Park, WY 82190-0168, and request an official map be sent to you. Lastly (and this one is NOT recommended), you could wait until you arrive and just ask us for a park map at the visitor center counter. But if you opt for the internet method and download a .pdf version of the map and print it out, you'll have the entire park on just one piece of paper, and it's a LOT easier to work with.

With your map in hand, the next step in ranger pre-planning is to locate the "Mark On Your Map" section at the start of the Two Day Ranger Plan and highlight those areas on your map with a colored marker so you'll have a better idea of where you'll be going. This will allow you to identify which features of the park you'll need to be nearest. It will also help you with the next step – locating lodging.

After you get a bead on where in the park you'll be visiting, the next sensible step is to start the process of figuring out your lodging. Where are you going to stay? Maybe you'd like to stay in a hotel, cabin, or an inn inside the park. Maybe you're OK with being just outside the park in lodging. Maybe you're trying to camp in one of the eleven campgrounds inside the park or the few campgrounds near any of the five entrance gates to the park. Whatever your lodging preference, now is the time to make reservations so you'll have a better experience. You'll see in the plans that there are places to stay inside the park, but you'll have to contact the lodging concessionaire, Xanterra, to make those reservations.

This next part is kind of sad. I can't tell you how many times visitors have stepped up to the visitor center desk and have no place to stay. In the middle of the very busy summer season, this is a recipe for disaster. People can make lodging reservations up to a year in advance. Many do. That means the best prices and the best locations are no longer available. It also means that without reservations, you'll be staying a long way away from the park and spend even more time just driving to the park entrance each day, not to mention the long drives inside the park. Don't do this to yourself. Plan ahead and make those reservations.

At the beginning of each plan, I use small icons to help guide you to features in the park you'll want to see and experience, as well as services that are near each stop you make. Use them to be sure you see everything there is at each location. Use them to know which park features are in each place and if there are restroom facilities, dining, gas stations, a postal facility, etc. in that part of the park. I have also included cautionary notices you should be aware of in each area. In my experience, people mark a slash through each feature to keep track of where they are and what they've seen. This seems to work well for most people. If that works for you, go for it.

The last part of your plan involves how you'll get to the vicinity of the park. By that I mean, are you flying in to one of the many airports in the area? Are you driving all the way to the park? Are you doing a combination of the two – flying and renting an automobile? Are you driving to the park and planning to camp inside the park? Are you driving an RV into the park? Whatever your means for getting to the park will probably involve some reservations as well. Make those reservations now, too, so you'll have the best time you could imagine.

Read on ... plan ... reserve ... and I hope you enjoy yourself.

Chapter Three

Challenges to Your Visit

Most visitors come to the visitor center desk and ask us to show them the best and most popular features of the park. Imagine that!! They've done no planning whatsoever and have no idea where things are or even what they could go and see, and they've only heard that Yellowstone National Park is a great place to visit. Well they're right, it IS a great place to visit, under the right circumstances. Here's what can happen – three sets of circumstances.

The first scenario goes like this. The visitor wants to see everything in the park – all the special places – and they only have the balance of the day and the next day. A total of a day and a half. Most tell us that they've planned their visit based upon what others have done in the park. They've found out from social media that you can see everything in the park in a day or so – IF you really concentrate on it. Please don't rely on information from social media. Most of it is wrong. These visitors are misinformed and in trouble, and they're going to have to pick something to skip. The park is just too big and the features are spread out way too far for them to get all of the sights in with only a day and a half – not going the maximum 45 MPH [72 KPH] legal speed limit in the park anyway. They're usually mortified when we tell them this, because they actually had no idea. They hadn't done any research (other than maybe a social media search on their cell phones on the way to the park), let alone any planning months before when they could have also had hotel reservations. They come to the park with no reservations and have no place to stay, thinking they can just find a room at the last minute. Now we realize that some people just can't get away for any more time than they've allowed, so something has to give. We usually try and get them to focus on one of the 'big three' (animals, geothermal or waterfalls) and take it from there. So we'll ask them if they're more interested in seeing animals, geo-thermal features like hot springs and geysers, or are they more focused on waterfalls. The answer we usually get back is "Well, we want to see it all." But that's not possible. At this juncture is when we usually point to the park map and explain from the west gate to the east gate is almost a three hour drive. That usually takes care of visitors understanding the timing issue as well as gives them a concept of how big Yellowstone is. From there, depending upon which of the 'big three' they want to focus on, we guide them to the best of the best and, admittedly, will skip other features. If they only had this book to help them plan their visit! Very simple.

The second scenario plays out like this. They have plenty of time, say, four or five days and they have reservations at a local hotel either inside or outside the park. This is our best visitor. This is the visitor we want to walk up to our visitor center desk (not that we wouldn't help the others). This is the visitor that'll realize after they leave the park that they really had a nice time and saw some of the most memorable things they ever thought they'd see. They've set aside enough time to see the major features of the park without having to scurry all over the place in a big hurry all the time, like people who have less time. They can take their time and really soak up and enjoy the park like it should be enjoyed. They'll get to see all of the best things about Yellowstone National Park. So when a visitor walks up to the desk and they tell me they have four or five days to see the park, I usually high-five them and thank them for having set aside the time. That also makes the planning of what they want to see and do go much better. They'll pretty much see everything and actually enjoy Yellowstone National Park.

The scenario for the number three group is in the vast minority, thankfully. The last scenario plays out like this. This type of visitor comes to the park, sneaks around and camps in the park without paying any fees, without paying attention to other visitors, and without caring what other people think of them. They're there just to take, and take, and take. They probably even have some contact with our law enforcement rangers. I don't think I need to say it very loudly but we don't care much for these type of visitors. We'd just as soon have them stay at home and watch a Yellowstone National Park DVD. Please try hard NOT to be this type of visitor.

So those are the three scenarios.

From there, you'll have other challenges as well. As of this writing, I've spent many seasons in Yellowstone National Park and have yet to see all the park has to offer. I'm there for about five and a half months at a time and still haven't seen everything. You can spend a lifetime there and not accomplish this. So my goal is to always do the best I can with whatever the visitor gives me to work with, and I know all my ranger buddies do the same. Isn't that what interpretation rangers should be doing anyway? Of course it is.

When you get into the Ranger Day Plans you'll see I used the terms "walk" and "hike." A walk is simply a short distance you'll cover to get to a particular feature and is usually less than a hundred yards, or about 91 meters or so, and fairly level. A hike, on the other hand, can be much further. The hikes are mostly in the longer Ranger Day Plans, and I encourage you to check at the trailhead for the distances and the difficulty before you try them. You can always check at a visitor center for hiking information as well.

Along with walking and hiking you may also have physical limitations that you're dealing with. The park is reasonably easy to get around in depending upon what you're trying to do. Please use common sense in these instances. All the major features are pretty easy to get to even with a handicap. Visitor centers in the park have Handicap Access Guides you can *borrow* to help give you guidance on where you can go with physical limitations. Remember that Handicap Access

Guides are *loaned* to you so please return them to any visitor center when you're done with your stay. Thank you.

CROWDS. Increasing visitation numbers that Yellowstone Park has been experiencing the last few years will slow you down as well. The park is not designed to handle the massive number of visitors that come each season. Simply put, since the park is designed for about two million visitors during a normal season, and the park is running at just over four million people per season, the park is two hundred percent overloaded. This means a normal parking lot designed for one hundred automobiles would have about two hundred cars trying to fit into those one hundred spaces. I don't care if you're into 'new math' or not, those cars are NOT going to fit into that parking lot. No how ... no way. So that means there are tons of cars parked helter skelter all over the place with long walks into and out of the features you're trying to see. It also means there are twice the number of people when you do finally get to the feature you're trying to see. That makes it tougher to take good pictures, more difficult to use restroom facilities, and more of a challenge to get out of the parking lot and down the road to the next feature. Do you see where this might cause delays and frustration with visitors? Of course, it does. And God help you if you don't have enough time to see the park. Can you begin to see why pre-planning is important here? I hope so.

ANIMAL JAMS. This next visitation challenge is

impossible to predict. We have large numbers of wild animals (and I emphasize WILD) inside the park. It's a known fact you can only see about two percent of the park from your vehicle. That means the animals have the other ninety-eight percent of the park to roam around in without you even seeing them. So when wild animals do get close to the roads – which you can almost assuredly bet on – there will be huge traffic jams, because all the visitors are trying to get the perfect picture. This happens way too often and can really mess you up trying to get to the next stop on your visitation plan. The worst of it is, you sit in heavy stopped traffic without moving at all for long periods of time. Then the traffic starts to roll along a bit better, and you get to the spot where the animal was, and it's strolled away, and you don't even see it. You scratch your head and wonder what was all the traffic for? So the only thing that's happened to you is that you're now spending way more time than you thought trying to get to your next stop. Can you see how pre-planning your visit might be of some value?

SAFETY. It's always a challenge for a ranger to keep the visitors safe while in any national park. Yellowstone is no different, and if anything, more of a challenge because of the huge diversity of things to do and see. So let's talk about safety in the park for a bit.

People that visit Yellowstone must take it upon themselves to keep themselves safe. The ultimate challenge for rangers, is for these same visitors to recognize that they're in an UNSAFE situation. This can, and does, happen very easily in Yellowstone.

We have animals – WILD animals – that can injure visitors or take a life. Visitors have some sort of compulsion to get way too close to the wild animals, usually to get that perfect up-close picture. Every season people are injured because the animals don't know anything more than you're invading their 'safe' zone. So they attack you as part of their 'fight or flight' response because you're getting too close. So the park has rules on how close you can be to ALL wild animals. Those guidelines are, 100 yards [91 meters] from bears and wolves, and 25 yards [23 meters] from ALL OTHER ANIMALS. So, no selfies with the bison or elk. Stop crowding around the animals, reasoning that "Hey that guy over there is WAY closer than I am, so I think I'll step a few feet closer." Next thing that happens is the animal retaliates for fear of too little space. Fight or flight! So please follow those distance rules and keep your distance. Thanks.

We have hydro-thermal and geo-thermal geyser basins that are deadly. That's why the park service built the boardwalks – to keep visitors safe. Virtually all of the geyser basins have a thin layer of geyserite surrounding them. Geyserite is a form of opaline silica that is often found around hot springs and geysers, and is sometimes very thin and cannot support much weight. Super-heated water is just under the surface. If the geyserite crumbles from your body weight, you're toast! Think about a bubbling and boiling pot of super-heated water on your stove. Toss in a hot dog. You're the hot dog! It isn't pretty. Yet people do this to themselves almost every season. Stay on the boardwalks! That's why the park service built them – for your safety in and around the geyser basins and thermal areas. Please don't step off a boardwalk for ANY reason. Thank you.

Yellowstone National Park is also very popular. We have loads of people from all over the world all trying to see and do the same things. This creates overcrowding situations that can end poorly. There's either resource damage from too many vehicles parked out of designated parking areas, or personal safety is compromised when a drivers attention is distracted by an animal and they allow their car to cross over the center line and create a head-on crash. Either way, this isn't a good outcome. If you as a visitor would just think about your situation and keep yourself safe in all cases, that would make us as rangers more at ease as well. Thank you.

COMMUNICATION. This challenge is mostly just an inconvenience. People aren't used to using maps much anymore. They want to plug the coordinates into their cell phones and away they go. Since there isn't much cell service in the park, this is a problem. Cell phone GPS works by being able to communicate with a cell tower. As of this writing, there are only three areas in the park where your cell phone works, so communicating with others is pretty limited. The cell phone areas are as follows: in and around Mammoth Hot Springs, the Old Faithful area, and some signal is available near the Canyon area of the park. In the rest of the park – which is the vast majority of the park – cell phone GPS is non-existent. So you'll have to rely on good old map skills to navigate around inside the park. OR … maybe just use this book?

WEATHER. Let's explain this challenge by giving you a couple of examples. Some people come to the desk and want to know where Grand Prismatic Spring is because they want to take a picture of it. That's great, except the day is very cool, maybe only in the low fifty degree range, and the spring is very hot. That means there will be loads of steam coming out of the spring because of the temperature differential. It's difficult to keep your camera lens – on your cell phone or otherwise – from fogging up from the steam. This makes for a less than desirable picture. As well, if it's raining and you try and go to the Canyon Village area to take a picture of Lower Falls, there are so many raindrops between where you are at the viewing area and the waterfall itself, that your picture will be 'fuzzed up' and out of focus from the precipitation. In addition, we get summer thunderstorms that roll through the park. It can rain buckets and mess up trail hiking as well as the boardwalks around the thermal features. We've even had snow in the middle of the summer. You never know what you'll get with the weather. There is just no way to plan for it.

Chapter Four

What the Symbols Mean

MAXIMUM speed limit – OR LESS - in the park!

This symbol represents a "Map Tip." On the official park map you'll notice a small box around this area of the park. This indicates there is a blow-up of the area at the top of the park map. Please look at the blow-up area for additional details of what's available to see and do in each area. Food, lodging, gasoline, and gift shops are available in these areas of the park during the peak season.

This is the icon for a major park feature. The park is loaded with features, and if you're not careful you can miss one or more. So I added this icon into the "Features" tab in each stop in the plan to let you know there is a major feature in that location.

This is a driving tip. These tips help you navigate around the park. They may also be something as simple as "watch out" for this or that, or more meaningful as "don't do" this or that.

 Caution: This area of the park is hydrothermally and geo-thermally active. PLEASE STAY ON THE BOARDWALKS AND DON'T TOUCH THE GEYSER WATER RUNOFF AS IT MAY HAVE ACID IN IT. PETS ARE NOT ALLOWED AND SMOKING IS NOT ALLOWED IN ANY OF THESE HYDRO-THERMAL OR SURROUNDING AREAS. Keep garbage and refuse in your pocket and dispose of in park garbage cans. Thank you.

I used this icon to let you know that you're in an area that you should exercise an abundance of caution as there are animals in the park that can injure you, or worse. One of those animals is a bear. Bear spray is 92 percent effective at stopping a bear attack when used properly. Because Yellowstone Park is full of wild animals, any time you are on a trail and getting away from other people out on your own, you need to be conscious of wild animals. Plain and simple, they can hurt you. If there are just two in your group, you should consider having bear spray with you. If there are three or more in your group, then bear spray – even though it's still a good idea – may not be necessary. It's up to you. Check the park newspaper you received when you entered the park for more details. Keep in mind a couple of things. If you flew to Yellowstone in a commercial aircraft and you purchase bear spray in the park, you will NOT be able to take the bear spray home with you. TSA will take it away. If you drove from home to the park, then you can just take it home with you. You can also rent bear spray during the summer season at the Canyon

Visitor Center (this is a private contractor to the park who may, or may not, rent bear spray each season). Either way, bear spray can save your life if you end up being too close to a wild animal. Just because it says 'bear spray' does NOT limit it to stopping other animals. Anything that breathes will be affected by the spray. That includes humans. So think about it, talk to a ranger if that helps you, and you decide what level of protection you need. If you purchase bear spray and can't take it home with you, you can always turn it in to any of the nine visitor centers in the park and we will take care of it for you. It's still up to you.

I used this symbol to let you know about additional information in this area of the park.

This is a stop number icon. I used this symbol to let you know how many features in an area of the park you should be looking for. Each feature has a number. In this case, there would only be one feature. If the number inside the stop sign image was a 6, then there are six things to do or see in that particular part of the park.

This icon means you may encounter an "Unapproved Area" of the park. Do not go further. This is a closed area.

 NO Large Vehicles. This symbol denotes

that an area of the park does NOT ALLOW large vehicles including Recreational Vehicles (RVs), trailers of any kind, dually trucks, or buses. They are prohibited in this area.

This area does NOT allow pets. Be very cautious and watch for "No Pets" signs in and around the entrance to ALL areas of the park including park trailheads. Please do not take your pet into these areas. Pets are allowed within 100 feet [30 meters] of a developed area such as roads, parking lots, campgrounds, and picnic areas unless posted otherwise. Please pick up after your pet. Thank you.

Do not smoke or use smoking products in these areas of the park.

This area contains one or more geysers. Remember to adhere to the caution guidelines and stay ON the boardwalks as you view geysers. Geysers contain extremely HOT water and can easily burn you. Most also contain concentrations of acid and may give you a chemical burn. So stay on those boardwalks! PLEASE!

This symbol denotes a hot spring. Hot springs are just that – they're HOT. Don't touch or get near hot springs. They can kill. Follow the caution guidelines and stay ON the boardwalks as you view hot springs.

This icon represents a waterfall. There is an active waterfall in this area of the park.

This icon represents bubbling mud. In this area of the park there are active bubbling mud area(s). Bubbling mud usually indicates the presence of large concentrations of acids. It is acid that broke the rock down to make the mud. So it follows not to touch the mud. Follow the caution guidelines and stay ON the boardwalks as you view bubbling mud areas.

This is an area that includes a photographic opportunity. Take those pictures! Have that memory!

This is the symbol for a National Park Service Visitor Center or Information Station. There are nine visitor centers or information stations within the park. Two have museums in them. They're located at Mammoth Hot Springs, Norris Geyser Basin, the town of West Yellowstone, Madison Junction, Old Faithful, Canyon Village, Fishing Bridge, Grant Village, and West Thumb Geyser Basin.

This area is frequented by rangers. Please feel free to ask any of us questions about the area, questions about the park, and remember to be on your best behavior as we're also watching you as well. Thank you.

There are restroom facilities in this area of the park.

This symbol indicates there is a gas station in the area.

This is the symbol for a medical clinic within the park.

This is the symbol for drinking water that is available in this vicinity of the park. Drinking water is actually available in a number of areas throughout the park and in some cases there are so many areas I was unable to list them all.

This icon tells you there is a dining area, restaurant, cafeteria or delicatessen at this location inside the park.

This is the icon for a grocery store inside the park.

This symbol means there is a gift shop or shopping available in this particular area of the park.

This is the symbol I used to indicate that a

U.S. Post Office facility is nearby.

This is the icon for a lodging facility in this part of the park. It may be a hotel, an inn, a lodge or cabins. The lodging in Yellowstone is managed by Xanterra on a reservation only basis. Xanterra can be contacted at 307-344-7311.

There is camping in this area of the park. It can be tent camping, pop-up trailer style camping, or some (and I emphasize 'some') campsites that can handle smaller RVs. Be aware that not all the campgrounds can be reserved as some are first-come first-serve facilities. Madison, Bridge Bay, Canyon, and Grant Village all require reservations, especially in the summer. The camping there is managed by Xanterra on a reservation only basis. Xanterra can be contacted at 307-344-7311.

This area is set aside for hard-sided camping only. This would include Class C and Class A motorhomes and RVs, but NOT tent trailers, tents or backpacking style camping. The only area of the park that can handle hard-sided RVs is Fishing Bridge RV Park. The camping here is managed by Xanterra on a reservation only basis. Xanterra can be contacted at 307-344-7311.

In this area there is a picnic spot. Actually in most areas there are multiple areas to picnic. Just be aware that bears can smell quite a long distance. So your very aromatic meal could be their aromatic meal.

There is an amphitheater in this area of the park. They're located at Mammoth Hot Springs, Madison Junction, Canyon Village, Fishing Bridge, Bridge Bay, and Grant Village. There are nightly ranger-led power point presentations about historical, natural, hydrothermal, cultural, or animal related topics in the park. The programs begin at dusk and start times vary with the season, so check at one of the visitor centers for the times. There is also a community room in the visitor center in the town of West Yellowstone that does ranger-led power point presentations. You can check for the times in the green section in the middle of the park newspaper available when you enter the park, or you can pick one up at a visitor center.

This is the symbol for hike or a trailhead. There are one or more trailheads in this area of the park. Remember that whenever you're on a trail to please carry sufficient water to keep yourself and others in your group hydrated sufficiently. This is your responsibility.

This area is one of nine National Park Service Visitor Centers or Information Stations in the park that operate the Junior Ranger Program. They're located at Mammoth Hot Springs, Norris Geyser Basin, the town of West Yellowstone, Madison Junction, Old Faithful, Canyon Village, Fishing Bridge, Grant Village, and West Thumb Geyser Basin. You can purchase the Junior Ranger materials for a nominal fee, and a ranger can explain how the program works to your child/children. Age range is from 4 years to 13+ years of age, but actually it's fun for the whole family. There is also a Young Adventurer program run from the Canyon Visitor Education Center. And the Young Scientist program where your child – or you, for that matter – can learn about hydro-thermal and geo-thermal activity run from the Old Faithful Visitor Education Center.

Mark On Your Map

With each Ranger Day Plan I included a list of the features your plan will allow you to see in the time you have. Mark these areas with a highlighter on your copy of the park map. This will assist you in knowing where you're going to on your Ranger Day Plan. I provide map guides with each of the four Ranger Day Plans to assist you in locating where the features are in the park that are on your Ranger Day Plan.

Features

Every area in any of the Ranger Day Plans will show features of the park that you'll want to take the time to see. After the 'Features' tag, you'll see a list of the things you can see and do in that area of the park.

Services

This tag will show you where additional services are located in that part of the park. These include places like visitor centers, restrooms, dining, gift shops, postal facilities and medical clinics.

Cautions

This tag shows you where features in the park can be very dangerous if you don't follow park rules. Keep your distance from hot springs, geysers, and steam vents. Watch out for wild animals and keep the prescribed and legal distance away from these animals. That's 100 yards [91 meters] from bears and wolves and 25 yards [23 meters] from ALL OTHER ANIMALS. Pets of any kind are NOT allowed on any boardwalks, areas near thermal features, and some trails. Look for signs at the start of these features. There is No Smoking near ANY thermal feature in the park. Stay on the boardwalks! These 'Cautions' are there to keep you from having an unwanted conversation with a Law Enforcement Ranger. Thank you for paying attention to this.

It's also worth noting, at this point, that as hard as I try, things change in the park. The information in this book reflects current conditions in the park which can change from time to time. When things change, I'll update this book in subsequent editions.

Chapter Five

How to See the Best of Yellowstone Park

DAY TRIP PLANNING

OK ... so let's go see some stuff!

As any ranger would do for you, this book is all about trip planning to help out those who want to come to Yellowstone but have no idea of where to begin. Remember that pre-trip planning is the best way to see everything you have the time for. There is no other way to accomplish this. All of the Ranger Day Plans include the best and the most spectacular places. Can you do me a favor though? Please don't make a VERY common mistake by trying to cut your time short by squeezing in too much, as you'll only get frustrated. If you only have two days set aside for seeing Yellowstone, don't try and use the four day plan and squeeze the four day plan into those two days. As I've said before, the park is just too big, the features are way too far apart, and you'll only exasperate yourself and guess what ... it's just not going to happen. If you want to use the four day plan, that's fine, but plan to stay for four days. Then it will work. Please take the advice of this experienced ranger, which is the same as we would give you if you were standing right in front of us at the visitor center desk ... don't try to squeeze in too much. Follow the Ranger Day Plans. Thanks.

The best plan of attack on planning your visit, is to get

hold of the official park map. As I mentioned earlier, you can go to

https://www.nps.gov/yell/planyourvisit/upload/YEL L_Tear-Off_Map2016.pdf

which is the official website for Yellowstone National Park and locate the park map. There is a .pdf of it available. Print out the map before you come to the park using the website OR wait until we hand you a map which comes with a park pass. Then highlight the areas from whichever Ranger Day Plan matches the number of days you have in the park. You now know where you're going.

Also, these Ranger Day Plans assume you are staying somewhat close to one of the park entrances or maybe even inside the park and not fifty miles [eighty kilometers] (or more) away from the park. People sometimes rationalize that staying further away from the park is more economical, and it probably is. But staying that far away from the park to save some money on hotel charges, only to discover they spend that extra savings on more fuel, higher rental car fees, and lost time in the park just to save a few bucks isn't always the smartest thing you can do. In most cases it isn't the wisest thing either. All you've accomplished is aggravation for yourself. You're on vacation. Enjoy yourself. Plan ahead, get reservations, and stay in or near the park.

Another thing, the stops at each feature are in no particular order as I can't predict which gate you'll use to enter the park. Just select a plan that fits the time-frame you set aside for your visit then, using the highlighted park map as your guide, start at the park feature in that plan that's closest to the gate you enter the park. Do as many features as you feel like on the first day, then pick up on the next day where you left off. I purposely left space on the left side of each stop in every plan so you can take notes and mark off those places you've seen. The park is arranged in two loops – Upper Grand Loop Road and Lower Grand Loop Road – so it's pretty hard to get lost. The two roads form a figure "8" and together are called the Grand Loop Road. So you should be able to pick up right where you left off the day before in the middle of your Ranger Day Plan.

Also, when you have the official park map in hand, notice there are five boxes at the top of the map on the park map side of the map. All five of these expanded areas (Mammoth Hot Springs; Old Faithful; Canyon Village; West Thumb, Grant Village, and Fishing Bridge; Lake Village and Bridge Bay) have gas, food, lodging, visitor centers and, yes, gift shops. So if you need any of these services, other than from the towns just outside the park, refer to these five expanded boxes to find those services inside the park.

What I have allowed for in the Ranger Day Plans are time for you to eat, time if you get in minor traffic jams, time to locate parking when it's a challenge, time to take a normal amount of photographs, and time to see the features of the park and actually enjoy them. I tried very diligently to build in this time just as we would at the visitor desk. Another consideration ... the fuel is more expensive inside the park and more than a few people have come to us when they've gotten too low on fuel and paid dearly for the Yellowstone Park Service vehicle to meet them for gas. You might think about topping off your fuel tank before entering the park each day. Remember, it's a BIG place.

Another point to consider, the shorter plans don't really have time to do things like the Junior Ranger, Young Scientist, or the Young Adventurer programs all designed for kids. With little time available to visit different areas of the park, think about the trade-off of spending your time seeing the natural features of the park. Of course, this is up to you.

Remember that during the peak summer season the entrance gates get backed up too. If you can get up early you can avoid lots of it. If you can enter the gate later in the morning and stay later in the day you'll avoid lots of it too. Think about it. Again it's up to you.

Lastly, there is no way to predict when a wild animal will get close enough to one of the main roads which destroys traffic flow. Everyone wants a picture or ten. Right? I mentioned this earlier in the 'challenges' chapter. This clogs up the roads fiercely. The plans do NOT have this excess time calculated into them even though the animal jams almost always happen. So try to get into an entrance gate as early each day as you can to avoid the animal jams taking up your whole day. The park is open 24/7 so getting in a gate should be easy with your park pass. Also, people get WAY TOO CLOSE to wild animals to try and get that perfect shot. *Please don't do this.* The park MINIMUMS are 100 yards [91 meters] from bears and wolves and 25 yards [23 meters] from all other animals. You CAN get injured, or worse. Remember, these are the park MINIMUMS! Please stay back. If the animal moves closer to you ... move back ... to maintain the minimum distance! When trying to take photos of your favorite animal, be sure to park your car with all FOUR tires past the white line at the edge of the roadway or you can be cited for impeding traffic flow. Be safe and be smart.

So let's get started on some planning ...

Chapter Six

1 Day Ranger Plan

With only one day to see the park you're going to have a pretty big challenge just seeing the best of the best (geysers, hot springs, a BIG waterfall, and some wild animals – NO HIKES – you just don't have enough time).

Mark On Your Map

Old Faithful, Grand Prismatic Spring, Fountain Paint Pots, Gibbon Falls, Beryl Spring, Virginia Cascades, Canyon Village Area, and Hayden Valley, all on the Lower Grand Loop Road. You may be able to see Mud Volcano, Sulphur Caldron, and the Fishing Bridge Area, depending upon daylight and the amount of time you have left in your day.

Use the map guide on the next page.

1 Day Ranger Plan

Mark the Ranger Day Plan stops shown here onto the park map you downloaded from the internet.

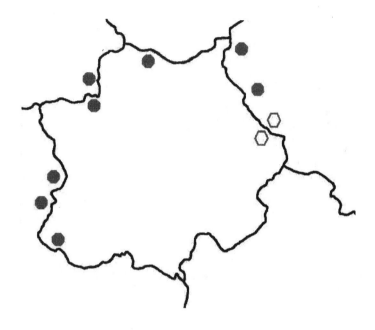

Lower Grand Loop Road

● This indicates a park feature you should highlight on a park map

⬡ This indicates a park feature you MAY NOT have the time to see based upon the time you have allowed.

Old Faithful
(Upper Geyser Basin):

Look on the park map you highlighted, locate Old Faithful Geyser, and drive to this area. As you head south, or north, on Lower Grand Loop Road, you'll come across an exit that looks much like a freeway exit back home. Follow the sign for Old Faithful and exit to the east. Your adventure has begun!

There is a National Park Service Visitor Education Center in this part of the park. During the summer visitation season there are National Park Service rangers who can help guide you to anywhere in the park you'd like to go. Just stop in and ask.

The main focus of the Old Faithful Visitor Education Center focuses around the geology that created Yellowstone National Park. From fumaroles, to steam vents, to geysers, to bubbling mud, to the volcano itself. Stop in and take a few minutes to wrap your mind around the catastrophic events that shaped the park.

(1) 🌳 You HAVE to take in Old Faithful Geyser. Why? Because it's Old Faithful Geyser, that's why. The geyser erupts about every 96 minutes – plus or minus 10 minutes. Each geyser eruption is dependent on the previous eruption so don't expect us to give you a "schedule." This is NOT an automated process where we push a button or use a computer for each eruption. This is totally natural and dependent on the super-heated water beneath. You can stop in at any visitor center and the rangers there will be glad to give you the next eruption time. This is one of the more important things we do. Take pictures.

(I) 🚶 This area is one of nine locations in the park that operate the Junior Ranger Program. There is a National Park Service Visitor Center in this area where you can purchase the Junior Ranger materials for a nominal fee. A ranger can explain how the program works to your child/children. Age range is from 4 years to 13+ years of age, but it's actually fun for the whole family. So don't let age stop you from participating in the very popular Junior Ranger program. It's great!!

🚗 Drive out of the Old Faithful area by exiting the parking area to your right and follow the road back to the overpass area. At the overpass area, exit to your right again, and head north.

Grand Prismatic Spring
(Midway Geyser Basin):

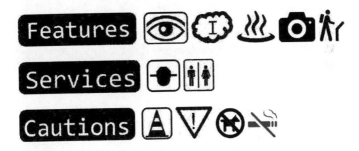

🚗 As you head north on the Lower Grand Loop Road, start looking to your left for the Grand Prismatic Spring parking area.

ℹ️ The parking lot here is grossly under-sized for the number of visitors to this area, so you'll have a challenge during peak usage times of the day getting a legal parking space. Please DO NOT park your car illegally as it may result in a parking citation. Thank you.

① As you walk from your car, you'll cross a bridge over the Firehole River. Stand on the bridge for a few minutes. Look up and down the river. Notice that the river is smaller upstream than it is downstream. This is because Excelsior Geyser (up the rise from where the huge water flows are entering the river) is dumping approximately 4,000 gallons [15,142 liters] of super-heated water right into the Firehole River every minute. This increases the volume of the river, making it wider. It also increases the temperature of the water and there are times during the summer season when there is algae in the water north of the bridge (downstream) because of the increased temperature. Take pictures.

② At the top of the walkway just past the bridge is Excelsior Geyser. This very azure blue once active geyser now expels large volumes of water into the Firehole River. Please be mindful on windy days in this entire area to hold onto personal belongings such as hats, scarves, etc., as they can easily be blown right off you. It costs the park service lots of money to keep this geyser free of blown-in debris, and it wrecks the uniqueness of this place when hats, scarves, etc. are in everyone's photos. Thank you. Take pictures.

③ ♨ Continue up the boardwalk
where you'll come to the multi-colored Grand
Prismatic Spring. This is a major attraction in
the park. Again, hold onto your hats, scarves,
etc. On warmer, less windy days, the steam is
reduced and it's easier to see the spring itself.
The opposite is true on cooler days. The steam
will fog up your camera lens and eyeglasses in
a heartbeat, making it a challenge to take good
pictures. As with most other colorful hot
springs, it needs good sunlight for the best
photos so between about ten in the morning
and mid-afternoon sometime are the best
photo opportunities. STAY ON THE
BOARDWALK AND DON'T TOUCH THE
WATER!! Take pictures.

ⓘ 📷 It's common for people to want
to take a photo of Grand Prismatic Spring
from an elevated area. These types of photos
are in many publications. The problem with
this is the hillside has been unstable for years.
There has been significant damage to
resources and visitor safety concerns have also
been an issue for quite some time. Park
administration worked diligently to come up
with a solution to this dilemma. In a
collaborative effort between geologists, park
administration, trail crews from Montana
Conservation Corps and Yellowstone Youth
Conservation Corps, a new trail has been

completed to an overlook with a view of Grand Prismatic Spring and the Midway Geyser Basin. The new trail is 105 feet [32 meters] high and just over one half mile long from the Fairy Falls Trail. The Fairy Falls parking area has also been redone to allow parking near the trailhead. So it's now possible to take great pictures of the spring and be safe at the same time. Please stay on this new trail to avoid further resource damage and possible fines. Thank you.

When you're back in your car, turn left out of the Grand Prismatic Spring parking area and head north again on the Lower Grand Loop Road.

Fountain Paint Pots
(Lower Geyser Basin):

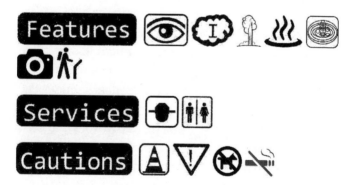

As you drive north, you'll see a sign for Fountain Paint Pots and Lower Geyser Basin. Turn left into the SOUTH end of this parking lot. Remember this entrance area as this is where you'll exit later.

The parking lot here is grossly under-sized for the number of visitors to this area, so you'll have a challenge during peak usage times of the day getting a legal parking space. Please DO NOT park your car illegally as it may result in a parking citation. Thank you.

1 As you walk up the boardwalk you'll come to Silex Spring on your right. Take pictures.

2 The next thing you'll see, up and to your left, is bubbling mud at Fountain Paint Pots. If you watch very carefully and stare at the middle of the bubbling pots, you'll see one or more pots actually spit up a small ball of molten mud about the size of a quarter. It happens about every minute or two. Don't get discouraged if nothing happens, because sometimes conditions are just not right. Take pictures.

3 Walk around and take in all the hot springs, steam vents (fumaroles), and small geysers in this area. Some are below and near the lower portion of the boardwalk when standing near Fountain Paint Pots. Walk down there. Take pictures.

4 Following the upper boardwalk near the Fountain Paint Pot feature, walk out the boardwalk to the west and down the stairs to Clepsydra Geyser. You'll witness a fairly regular eruption of hot steam and water that ejects out the top of this geyser. Take pictures.

When you're done visiting the Fountain Paint Pot area, drive to the SOUTH end of the parking area and exit the parking area by turning left (you can't turn left at the north end of the parking area). Continue heading north on the Lower Grand Loop Road.

Gibbon Falls:

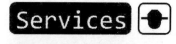

About six miles [nine kilometers] north of Madison Junction, you'll come to Gibbon Falls on the east side of the road. Turn right into the parking area.

(1) This is a pretty waterfall and a nice place to stretch your legs. It is also one of those areas that if you have an animal that needs to be walked, you can do so if you're never any further than 100 feet [30 meters] from a developed area. Be mindful of the distance though. Some people do go all the way down to the far end of the walkway to get a great picture but are well past the 100 feet [30 meters] maximum distance from the parking lot. Please pick up after your animal. It's also an area rangers like to rove around quite a bit more than some other areas and answer visitors' questions about the park. From this area, looking to the south along the ridges of the mountains, you can also see the remnants of the last volcanic eruption 640,000 years ago. Take pictures.

(i) If you need a restroom in this area of the park, there is no restroom right at Gibbon Falls. But just to the north up the road about a quarter mile on your left is Iron Spring picnic area, and there is a restroom there.

From the Gibbon Falls area, turn right out of the parking lot back onto the Lower Grand Loop Road and head north again.

Beryl Spring:

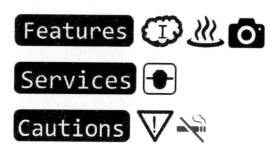

Beryl Spring is right along the roadway on the left side of the road, a few miles north of Gibbon Falls. You'll probably see the steam before you see the bridge or the spring. Pull off to the left side of the roadway and park your car.

The spring is just adjacent to the Gibbon River. The spring drains into the river and produces quite a bit of steam, even on moderately warm summer days. There is a short bridge right next to the spring, which can make the drive over the bridge with a vehicle a challenge because of the 'London fog' amounts of steam wafting right over the roadway on the bridge. The spring is on your left.

This is a short stop. Walk a couple of hundred feet [61 meters] up near the bridge, and enjoy one of Yellowstone's lesser viewed springs but a nice one just the same. Take pictures.

🚗 When you're done at Beryl Spring, continue driving north on the Lower Grand Loop Road to the Norris Geyser Basin intersection. Turn right at this large 4-way stop intersection and head east towards Canyon Village.

Virginia Cascades:

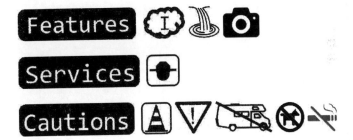

🚗 About five or six miles [about 8 or 9 kilometers] down the road from the Norris Geyser Basin intersection, you'll see a sign for Virginia Cascades Drive. With your normal sized vehicle, bear to the right (it's a slight "Y" intersection) onto the two mile, or so, one-way cascades drive.

This one-way road is a great little side jaunt but NO LARGE VEHICLES! If you're in a large vehicle just keep heading east toward Canyon Village. Please don't go in Virginia Cascades.

This short little road takes you

past one of the "cascade" style waterfalls in the park formed by multiple layers of lava flows thousands of years ago that created small shelves of volcanic rock that the Gibbon River runs over. It's like water running down a stairwell. This creates the effect referred to as a cascade. Take pictures.

When you're done at Virginia Cascades and at the end of the one-way drive, turn right to get back onto the Grand Loop Road and head east towards Canyon Village.

Canyon Village Area:

As you're coming into the Canyon Village area, turn right at the large 4-way stop intersection and drive south toward Fishing Bridge on the Lower Grand Loop Road.

There is a National Park Service Visitor Education Center in this part of the park. During the summer visitation season there are National Park Service rangers who can help guide you to anywhere in the park you'd like to go. Just stop in and ask.

The Canyon Village Visitor Education Center's main focus is all about the volcano. From the first eruption about 2.1 million years ago to the last eruption 640,000 years ago, this educational experience takes you all the way through. This is powerful. Take pictures.

Located in the Canyon Village area is the largest waterfall in the 'front country' area of the park. It's called Lower Falls and can be viewed best from Artist Point. The waterfall is 308 feet high, or 94 meters, and at its peak the average flow of the Yellowstone River is around 63,500 gallons per second, or for you metrically challenged folks, that's more than 240,000 liters per second. At some parts of the season the flow is much higher IF there has been an unusually high snowfall the previous winter.

The third left turn is called South Rim Drive with a sign saying "Artist Point." The parking lot for Artist Point – all the way at the end of this drive – is pretty good sized for automobiles and small RVs. Be careful if you're in a larger RV as there is limited parking for larger vehicles like RVs. This lot also fills to capacity during the busy summer months.

① 🌊 After parking in the main lot, walk to the east a couple of hundred yards [183 meters] over to the Lower Falls viewing platform which has a lower and upper viewing area to take pictures. This area IS handicap accessible. Take pictures.

⚠️ Don't stand on the stone walls as it's unsafe, a LONG way down, and probably not survivable.

💭 While at Artist Point you have a wonderful and dramatic view of Grand Canyon of the Yellowstone. At the viewing area between the waterfall and where you're standing is the start of the "grand canyon." If you walk around to the back side of the viewing area, you can see more of the canyon as it continues downstream. Take pictures.

🚗 🛗 Drive back the way you came on South Rim Drive out to the main Lower Grand Loop Road and turn right. Drive to that large 4-way stop intersection and turn right again. This will take you into the Canyon Village area on your right, where the National Park Service Visitor Center is located as well as food, restrooms, gift shops, a post office, and the lodges. This area IS handicap accessible. There is also a gas station, a campground, and an amphitheater in this area.

There is an amphitheater near the campground in this area of the park. There are nightly ranger-led power point presentations about historical, natural, hydrothermal, cultural, or animal related topics in the park. The programs begin at dusk and start times vary with the season, so check at one of the visitor centers for the times. You can also check for the times in the green section in the middle of the park newspaper available when you entered the park, or you can pick one up at a visitor center.

This area has one of nine locations in the park that operate the Junior Ranger Program. There is a National Park Service Visitor Center in Canyon Village where you can purchase the Junior Ranger materials for a nominal fee. A ranger can explain how the program works to your child/children. Age range is from 4 years to 13+ years of age, but it's actually fun for the whole family. So don't let age stop you from participating in the very popular Junior Ranger program. It's great!!

When you're done in the Canyon Village area, drive back out to that large 4-way stop intersection again and turn left. You'll be heading south on the Lower Grand Loop Road.

Hayden Valley:

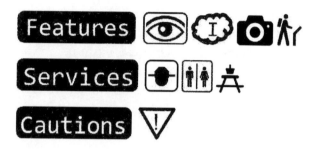

Features 👁 💭I 📷 🚶

Services ⊖ 🚻 ⛱

Cautions ⚠

🚗 Continue heading south from the Canyon Village area on the Lower Grand Loop Road. After going about three or four miles [six kilometers], you'll be entering the Hayden Valley area.

💭I Hayden Valley is named for Ferdinand Vandeveer Hayden who in 1871 led one of first surveys of Yellowstone National Park and the surrounding area. Hayden was a geologist and was federally funded to document the area for possible legislation to create the park.

①⚠ Hayden Valley has lots of WILD animals. The primary animals that roam this area are bison, elk, wolves and an occasional grizzly bear. Seasonally, there are sometimes black bear and moose in the area as well. You'll probably get into animal jams (traffic jams caused by animals) as visitors take photos of wild animals. Watch the car in front of you! Most times the animals are a ways away and easy to photograph. Sometimes they're right up on the roadway and people get WAY TOO CLOSE to them for their own safety. People DO get injured when attacked. Please stay a MINIMUM of 100 yards [91 meters] from bears and wolves and 25 yards [23 meters] away from ALL OTHER wild animals. Drive safely, keep your distance from animals, and take pictures.

You've been driving south on the Lower Grand Loop Road. Just keep driving south heading towards the Mud Volcano area.

Mud Volcano and Sulphur Caldron:
(From this part of the One Day Ranger Plan and ON – You MAY run out of daylight)

Park your car in the main Mud Volcano parking area. It will be just past the Sulphur Caldron area (on your left), but DON'T PARK in the Sulphur

Caldron parking area. Just continue down the road
about a hundred yards [91 meters] and the main lot
will be off to your right. It's a pretty good sized lot so
you shouldn't have too much trouble.

In this area there are two wonderful thermal
features – Mud Volcano and Sulphur Caldron. The
Mud Volcano area has a nice sized parking lot and it's
usually pretty easy to find parking in this area.

1 Walk up onto the small mountain
or large hill – whichever way you want to look
at it – and enjoy bubbling mud pots, small
caldrons, Dragon's Breath, fumaroles (steam
vents), and a whole array of other geo-thermal
and hydro-thermal features. You'll also enjoy
the aromatic odor of sulphur, thanks to
Mother Nature. The aromatic aroma in this
area is probably the strongest in the park.
Enjoy!

2 When you come down the Mud
Volcano hill on the boardwalk, you'll notice a
small parking lot on the opposite side of the
road and just a bit to the north that looks like
overflow parking for the main lot. Don't be
fooled! It is NOT overflow parking and many
people make the mistake of thinking it is – so
they take off and miss a wonderful feature of
the park. Just leave your car in the main Mud
Volcano parking lot and walk across the Lower
Grand Loop Road – WATCH OUT FOR

TRAFFIC – as people zip right through this area. After you're across the road, walk up a slight hill to your left and over to the stone wall and look down. You'll see two huge bubbling mud caldrons. This is Sulphur Caldron. Take pictures as this is a feature you'll be glad you didn't miss.

Please DO NOT take your RV (small or not) over to the parking area near Sulphur Caldron. There is limited parking there at best and an RV in this area will probably get blocked in by other vehicles. Please just walk over to Sulphur Caldron from the main parking lot at Mud Volcano. Thanks.

This is the end of this One Day Ranger Plan. I hope you had a good time, enjoyed the park, and are excited about coming back again soon. Thank you for following this plan.

Please drive safely when leaving the park.

NOTE FROM THE AUTHOR

Please do me a huge favor. IF you like this book and it helped you navigate your way around Yellowstone, please, please, please ... take a moment and let the world know through social media such as Facebook,

Twitter, email and text messaging, and please write a review. Thank you.

Chapter Seven

2 Day Ranger Plan

You still don't have too much time to see the park, but this Ranger Day Plan I put together to get you around to the best things along with a few surprises: (geysers, hot springs, bubbling mud, a BIG waterfall or two, and some wild animals).

Mark On Your Map Old Faithful, Grand Prismatic Spring, Firehole Lake Drive, Fountain Paint Pots, Gibbon Falls, Beryl Spring, Virginia Cascades, Canyon Village Area, Hayden Valley, Mud Volcano, Sulphur Caldron, Tower Fall Area, Tower-Roosevelt Area, Lamar Valley, Petrified Tree, Mammoth Hot Springs and the Upper Terraces. You may not be able to see Norris Geyser Basin, depending upon daylight and the amount of time you have left in your day.

Use the map guides on the next two pages.

2 Day Ranger Plan

Mark the Ranger Day Plan stops shown here onto the park map you downloaded from the internet.

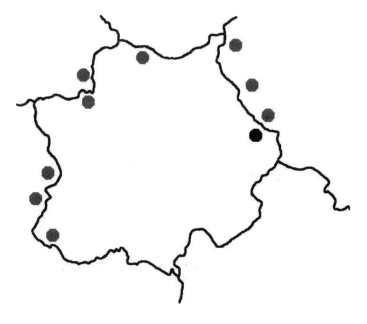

Lower Grand Loop Road

● This indicates a park feature you should highlight on a park map

Mark the Ranger Day Plan stops shown here onto the park map you downloaded from the internet.

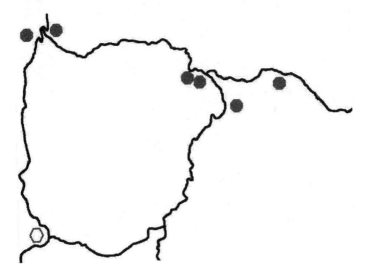

Upper Grand Loop Road

● This indicates a park feature you should highlight on a park map

⬡ This indicates a park feature you MAY NOT have the time to see based upon the time you have allowed.

Old Faithful
(Upper Geyser Basin):

Look on the park map you highlighted, locate Old Faithful Geyser, and drive to this area. As you head south, or north, on Lower Grand Loop Road, you'll come across an exit that looks much like a freeway exit back home. Follow the sign for Old Faithful and exit to the east. Your adventure has begun!

There is a National Park Service Visitor Education Center in this part of the park. During the summer visitation season there are National Park Service rangers who can help guide you to anywhere in the park you'd like to go. Just stop in and ask.

The main focus of the Old Faithful Visitor Education Center focuses around the geology that

created Yellowstone National Park. From fumaroles, to steam vents, to geysers, to bubbling mud, to the volcano itself. Stop in and take a few minutes to wrap your mind around the catastrophic events that shaped the park.

①🌲 You HAVE to take in Old Faithful Geyser. Why? Because it's Old Faithful Geyser, that's why. The geyser erupts about every 96 minutes – plus or minus 10 minutes. Each geyser eruption is dependent on the previous eruption so don't expect us to give you a "schedule." This is NOT an automated process where we push a button or use a computer for each eruption. This is totally natural and dependent on the super-heated water beneath. You can stop in at any visitor center and the rangers there will be glad to give you the next eruption time. This is one of the more important things we do. Take pictures.

②🚶 You have enough time to walk around behind Old Faithful Geyser and look for the sign leading you up to Observation Point. You'll have to time this for about a half hour before the next eruption of the geyser. This is a short hike up onto a hill that will give you a unique view of an Old Faithful eruption. When you get up to Observation Point, sit for a while and when the eruption is near, get those cameras ready. When Old Faithful

erupts, it will erupt up to your eye level instead of erupting up and away from you, as if you were down on the viewing platform by the geyser. So you'll be even with the top of the eruption. It's a pretty neat vantage point and worth the hike up the hill. Take pictures.

You'll see that you can also continue hiking out toward Solitary Geyser. Be careful not to burn up too much time. This hike is OK if you want to, but strongly consider having bear spray with you if you try to extend this hike on the hill any further than you have already gone. Not nearly as many people go out to Solitary Geyser as do the Observation Point hike. My take on it would be to skip going out to Solitary because of the time factor. Just think about your safety a bit and consider what danger you may be in. It's up to you.

You have time in this Ranger Day Plan so after you get down to the bottom of the hill again, continue walking around behind Old Faithful Geyser (stay on the trails and boardwalks). You'll see hundreds of other geo-thermal and hydro-thermal features behind Old Faithful up on Geyser Hill. Take pictures.

Walk over to the Old Faithful Inn – the building with a bunch of flags up on top. This is the structure that was saved from the fires of 1988 by hundreds of brave firefighters who basically put their backs to the building and any fire that was anywhere near them, they put it out. Thank you firefighters. Go into the lobby area; I'm not going to tell you where, but look for the clock. That's right ... the clock. Look around and if you can't see it, ask someone in Concierge or the gift shop where the clock is and when they show you, you'll be a bit embarrassed. It's one of those things that's right in front of your face and sometimes your eyes don't see it. Have fun with it. Take pictures.

Also, at the Old Faithful Inn, there is an outdoor viewing platform area (a parking area cover) above the drop-off area for cars and buses at the front of the building by the lobby. Go into the lobby area, walk to the back-left area of the lobby, and walk up the staircase. Walk forward and out the glass doors onto the viewing area. This is a good place to take a picnic lunch and view Old Faithful Geyser eruptions. You can bring your own packed lunch or buy prepared meals at the cafés or delicatessens in the Inn.

This area is one of nine locations in the park that operate the Junior Ranger Program. There is a National Park Service Visitor Center in this area where you can purchase the Junior Ranger materials for a nominal fee. A ranger can explain how the program works to your child/children. Age range is from 4 years to 13+ years of age, but it's actually fun for the whole family. So don't let age stop you from participating in the very popular Junior Ranger program. It's great!!

Old Faithful Inn is one of approximately 900 historic buildings in the park. It was originally built back in the early 1900s and boasts beautiful, breathtaking views of Old Faithful Geyser, hundreds of geothermal and hydrothermal features, surrounding mountain areas, and is a major lodging place in this area of the park. Want to stay in a famous and historic area of the park? This is one of those places. This major hotel has it all, from upscale rooms, the finest dining, gift shops, and evening entertainment during peak season. It has a large number of rooms. Lodging here is managed by Xanterra on a reservation only basis. Xanterra can be contacted at 307-344-7311. Take pictures.

Old Faithful Lodge is available for overnight stays and features nice rooms as well as eating and dining areas. It also has a large number of rooms. Lodging here is managed by Xanterra on a reservation only basis. Xanterra can be contacted at 307-344-7311. Take pictures.

I **bed** Snow Lodge is available for overnight stays and features nice rooms as well as eating and dining areas. It has numerous rooms and is also open during the winter season as well. Lodging here is managed by Xanterra on a reservation only basis. Xanterra can be contacted at 307-344-7311. Take pictures.

I There is no campground near the Old Faithful area.

car Drive out of the Old Faithful area by exiting the parking area to your right and follow the road back to the overpass area. Exit to your right again and head north.

Grand Prismatic Spring
(Midway Geyser Basin):

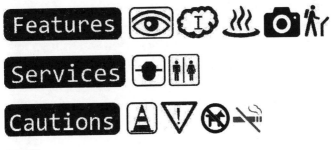

 As you head north on the Lower Grand Loop

Road, start looking to your left for the Grand Prismatic Spring parking area.

(I) The parking lot here is grossly under-sized for the number of visitors to this area, so you'll have a challenge during peak usage times of the day getting a legal parking space. Please DO NOT park your car illegally as it may result in a parking citation. Thank you.

(1) As you walk from your car, you'll cross a bridge over the Firehole River. Stand on the bridge for a few minutes. Look up and down the river. Notice that the river is smaller upstream than it is downstream. This is because Excelsior Geyser (up the rise from where the huge water flows are entering the river) is dumping approximately 4,000 gallons [15,142 liters] of super-heated water right into the Firehole River every minute. This increases the volume of the river making it wider. It also increases the temperature of the water and there are times during the summer season when there is algae in the water north of the bridge (downstream) because of the increased temperature. Take pictures.

(2) At the top of the walkway just past the bridge is Excelsior Geyser. This very azure blue once active geyser now expels large volumes of water into the Firehole River.

Please be mindful on windy days in this entire area to hold onto personal belongings such as hats, scarves, etc., as they can easily be blown right off you. It costs the park service lots of money to keep this geyser free of blown-in debris and it wrecks the uniqueness of this place when hats, scarves, etc are in everyone's photos. Thank you. Take pictures.

(3) ♨ Continue up the boardwalk where you'll come to the multi-colored Grand Prismatic Spring. This is a major attraction in the park. Again, hold onto your hats, scarves, etc. On warmer, less windy days, the steam is reduced and it's easier to see the spring itself. The opposite is true on cooler days. The steam will fog up your camera lens and eyeglasses in a heartbeat, making it a challenge to take good pictures. As with most other colorful hot springs, it needs good sunlight for the best photos so between about ten in the morning and mid-afternoon sometime are the best photo opportunities. STAY ON THE BOARDWALK AND DON'T TOUCH THE WATER!! Take pictures.

(I) 📷 It's common for people to want to take a photo of Grand Prismatic Spring from an elevated area. These types of photos are in many publications. The problem with this is the hillside has been unstable for years. There has been significant damage to resources and visitor safety concerns have also been an issue for quite some time. Park administration worked diligently to come up with a solution to this dilemma. In a collaborative effort between geologists, park administration, trail crews from Montana Conservation Corps and Yellowstone Youth Conservation Corps, a new trail has been completed to an overlook with a view of Grand Prismatic Spring and the Midway Geyser Basin. The new trail is 105 feet [32 meters] high and just over one half mile long from the Fairy Falls Trail. The Fairy Falls parking area has also been redone to allow parking near the trailhead. So it's now possible to take great pictures of the spring and be safe at the same time. Please stay on this new trail to avoid further resource damage and possible fines. Thank you.

When you're back in your car, turn left out of the Grand Prismatic Spring parking area and head north again on the Lower Grand Loop Road.

Firehole Lake Drive:

Cautions 🅐 ⚠️ 🚐 🚫🐾 🚭

🚗🚐 As you drive north from the Grand Prismatic Spring area, you'll see the sign for Firehole Lake Drive. Turn right IF you have a normal sized vehicle. Sorry ... NO large vehicles.

①🌳♨️ After making the right turn onto Firehole Lake Drive (in your regular sized vehicle), continue on. This drive includes going past more hydro-thermal and geo-thermal features including Great Fountain Geyser, White Dome Geyser, and Firehole Lake at the back end of this loop. Great Fountain Geyser doesn't erupt very often, but when it does ... it's spectacular. Eruption times are available at any of the visitor centers in the park. Take pictures.

🚗 At the end of this one-way drive you'll find yourself just across from Fountain Paint Pots. You'll also see you can't cut across the intersection legally to enter that area. SO, turn left at this intersection and go south for a couple hundred yards [183 meters], or so, and turn right into the far end of the parking area for Fountain Paint Pots. See how easy that was?

Fountain Paint Pots
(Lower Geyser Basin):

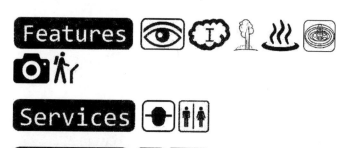

Features

Services

Cautions

As you drive north, you'll see a sign for Fountain Paint Pots and Lower Geyser Basin. Turn left into the SOUTH end of this parking lot. Remember this entrance area as this is where you'll exit later.

The parking lot here is grossly under-sized for the number of visitors to this area, so you'll have a challenge during peak usage times of the day getting a legal parking space. Please DO NOT park your car illegally as it may result in a parking citation. Thanks.

1. As you walk up the boardwalk you'll come to Silex Spring on your right. Take pictures.

2. The next thing you'll see, up and to your left, is bubbling mud at Fountain Paint

Pots. If you watch very carefully and stare at the middle of the bubbling pots, you'll see one or more pots actually spit up a small ball of molten mud about the size of a quarter. It happens about every minute or two. Don't get discouraged if nothing happens, because sometimes conditions are just not right. Take pictures.

3 Walk around and take in all the hot springs, steam vents (fumaroles), and small geysers in this area. Some are below and near the lower portion of the boardwalk when standing near Fountain Paint Pots. Walk down there. Take pictures.

4 Following the upper boardwalk near the Fountain Paint Pot feature, walk out the boardwalk to the west and down the stairs to Clepsydra Geyser. You'll witness a fairly regular eruption of hot steam and water that ejects out the top of this geyser. Take pictures.

When you're done visiting the Fountain Paint Pot area, drive to the SOUTH end of the parking area and exit the parking area by turning left (you can't turn left at the north end of the parking area). Continue heading north on the Lower Grand Loop Road.

Gibbon Falls:

Features

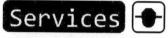

Services

Cautions

About six miles [9.5 kilometers] north of Madison Junction, you'll come to Gibbon Falls on the east side of the road. Turn right into the parking area.

This is a pretty waterfall and a nice place to stretch your legs. It is also one of those areas that if you have an animal that needs to be walked, you can do so if you're never any further than 100 feet [30 meters] from a developed area. Be mindful of the distance though. Some people do go all the way down to the far end of the walkway to get a great picture but are well past the 100 feet [30 meters] maximum distance from the parking lot. Please pick up after your animal. It's also an area rangers like to rove around quite a bit more than some other areas and answer visitors' questions about the park. From this area, looking to the south along the ridges of the mountains, you can also see the remnants of the last volcanic eruption

640,000 years ago. Take pictures.

 If you need a restroom in this area of the park, there is no restroom right at Gibbon Falls. But just to the north up the road about a quarter mile on your left is Iron Spring picnic area, and there is a restroom there.

From the Gibbon Falls area, turn right out of the parking lot back onto the Lower Grand Loop Road and head north again.

Beryl Spring:

Beryl Spring is right along the roadway on the left side of the road, a few miles north of Gibbon Falls. You'll probably see the steam before you see the bridge or the spring. Pull off to the left side of the roadway and park your car.

The spring is just adjacent to the Gibbon

River. The spring drains into the river and produces quite a bit of steam, even on moderately warm summer days. There is a short bridge right next to the spring, which can make the drive over the bridge with a vehicle a challenge because of the 'London fog' amounts of steam wafting right over the roadway on the bridge. The spring is on your left.

(1) ♨ This is a short stop. Walk a couple of hundred feet [61 meters] up near the bridge, and enjoy one of Yellowstone's lesser viewed springs but a nice one just the same. Take pictures.

🚗 From the Beryl Spring area, continue to drive north up to the Norris Geyser Basin intersection. Turn right at this large 4-way stop intersection and head east towards Canyon Village. Don't worry about Norris Geyser Basin right now as we'll come back to this area later on.

Virginia Cascades:

About five or six miles [9.5 kilometers] down the road from the Norris Geyser Basin intersection, you'll see a sign for Virginia Cascades Drive. With your normal sized vehicle, bear to the right (it's a slight "Y" intersection) onto the two mile, or so, one-way cascades drive.

This one-way road is a great little side jaunt but NO LARGE VEHICLES! If you're in a large vehicle just keep heading east toward Canyon Village. Please don't go in Virginia Cascades.

This short little road takes you past one of the "cascade" style waterfalls in the park formed by multiple layers of lava flows thousands of years ago that created small shelves of volcanic rock that the Gibbon River runs over. It's like water running down a stairwell. This creates the effect referred to as a cascade. Take pictures.

When you're done at Virginia Cascades and at the end of the one-way drive, turn right to get back onto the Grand Loop Road and head east towards Canyon Village.

Canyon Village Area:

Services

Cautions

As you're coming into the Canyon Village area, turn right at the large 4-way stop intersection and drive south toward Fishing Bridge on the Lower Grand Loop Road.

There is a National Park Service Visitor Education Center in this part of the park. During the summer visitation season there are National Park Service rangers who can help guide you to anywhere in the park you'd like to go. Just stop in and ask.

The Canyon Village Visitor Education Center's main focus is all about the volcano. From the first eruption about 2.1 million years ago to the last eruption 640,000 years ago, this educational experience takes you all the way through. This is powerful. Take pictures.

Located in the Canyon Village area is the largest waterfall in the 'front country' area of the park. It's called Lower Falls and can be viewed best from Artist Point. The waterfall is 308 feet high, or 94 meters, and at its peak the average flow of the Yellowstone River is around 63,500 gallons per second, or for you metrically challenged folks, that's more than 240,000 liters per second. At some parts of the season the flow is much higher IF there has been an unusually high snowfall the previous winter.

The third left turn is called South Rim Drive with a sign saying "Artist Point." The parking lot for Artist Point – all the way at the end of this drive – is pretty good sized for automobiles and small RVs. Be careful if you're in a larger RV as there is limited parking for larger vehicles like RVs and tour buses. This lot also fills to capacity during the busy summer months.

After parking in the main lot, walk to the east a couple of hundred yards [183 meters] over to the Lower Falls viewing platform which has a lower and upper viewing area to take pictures. This area IS handicap accessible. Take pictures.

Don't stand on the stone walls as it's unsafe, a LONG way down, and probably not survivable.

While at Artist Point you have a wonderful and dramatic view of Grand Canyon of the Yellowstone. At the viewing area between the waterfall and where you're standing is the start of the "grand canyon." If you walk around to the back side of the viewing area you can see more of the canyon as it continues downstream. Take pictures.

Drive back the way you came on South Rim Drive out to Lower Grand Loop Road and turn right. This will take you north again toward Canyon Village area. Turn right where the sign says "North Rim Drive" and "Brink of the Lower Falls." You'll see a parking lot right away. This is where you should try to park. This parking lot fills to capacity quite often so do the best you can.

②☖ The walkway is near the start of this parking lot on the south side. The hike down to Brink of the Lower Falls is challenging. It's about 250 to 300 feet [76 to 91 meters] down and the trail is a switchback style trail. But remember, you're at almost 8,000 feet [2,413 meters] elevation. Stand at the top of the trail and decide if you can make the journey. It's well worth it IF you can do it. Ask others that are coming back up how hard it was for them and make your decision from there. If you decide to go down, you'll be standing at the very top of the waterfall with all that water rushing right past you before it falls over the brink. It's pretty impressive. Take pictures.

Back in your car, continue to drive along North Rim Drive as it's a one-way road anyway. There are "Lookout Point" and "Grand View" viewing areas with good photo opportunities of Grand Canyon of the Yellowstone along the way. Why not stop as you can always delete the picture(s) later if you don't want them, right? As you continue along North Rim Drive, you'll also see the sign on your right for "Inspiration Point." Make the right turn and drive out to the parking lot at the end.

(3) Inspiration Point is another fantastic view up and down Grand Canyon of the Yellowstone. The Minnetaree Indians called the area "Mi tse a-da-zi," which means "Rock Yellow River." Yellowstone's version of the Grand Canyon in Arizona, is called Grand Canyon of the Yellowstone and is about 22 miles [35 kilometers] long and follows the Yellowstone River up to Tower Fall area, which we'll talk about later on. Take pictures.

Drive your car back to the intersection on the one-way road and turn right. As you continue to follow North Rim Drive, the one-way road will take you back to the Canyon Village area where the National Park Service Visitor Center is located as well as food, restrooms, gift shops, a post office, and the lodges. Most of these facilities will be on your left as you enter the area. This area IS handicap accessible. The gas station, campground, and amphitheater will be on your right.

You may be wondering why I have you back-tracking. This is because if you get to

Lower Falls too late in the day, the picture quality will go way down as the sun would be getting too close to the horizon and foul up your photos. Please forgive me.

There is an amphitheater near the campground in this area of the park. There are nightly ranger-led power point presentations about historical, natural, hydrothermal, cultural, or animal related topics in the park. The programs begin at dusk and start times vary with the season, so check at one of the visitor centers for the times. You can also check for the times in the green section in the middle of the park newspaper available when you entered the park, or you can pick one up at a visitor center.

This area has one of nine locations in the park that operate the Junior Ranger Program. There is a National Park Service Visitor Center in Canyon Village where you can purchase the Junior Ranger materials for a nominal fee. A ranger can explain how the program works to your child/children. Age range is from 4 years to 13+ years of age, but it's actually fun for the whole family. So don't let age stop you from participating in the very popular Junior Ranger program. It's great!!

The Canyon Village area has plenty of lodging available at Canyon Lodge but during the summer season everything is booked solid so if you want to stay in this part of the park you'll have to book early. Canyon Lodge just completed a major addition of hundreds of rooms that are brand new. This is a very popular place to stay in the park and reservations are a must during the busy season. Reservations can be made through Xanterra at 307-344-7311.

Canyon Village also has a nice campground complex. The campground here is located north of the main intersection near the gas station. Like Madison Campground, it too can handle some smaller RVs but is designed mostly for tent and tent trailer camping. Reservations can be made through Xanterra at 307-344-7311.

When you're done in the Canyon Village area, drive back out to that large 4-way stop intersection and turn left. You'll be heading south on the Lower Grand Loop Road.

Hayden Valley:

Cautions ⚠

Continue heading south from the Canyon Village area on the Lower Grand Loop Road. After going about three or four miles [six kilometers], you'll be entering the Hayden Valley area.

Hayden Valley is named for Ferdinand Vandeveer Hayden who in 1871 led one of first surveys of Yellowstone National Park and the surrounding area. Hayden was a geologist and was federally funded to document the area for possible legislation to create the park.

Hayden Valley has lots of WILD animals. The primary animals that roam this area are bison, elk, wolves and an occasional grizzly bear. Seasonally, there are sometimes black bear and moose in the area as well. You'll probably get into animal jams (traffic jams caused by animals) as visitors take photos of wild animals. Watch the car in front of you! Most times the animals are a ways away and easy to photograph. Sometimes they're right up on the roadway and people get WAY TOO CLOSE to them for their own safety. People DO get injured when attacked. Please stay a MINIMUM of 100 yards [91 meters] from bears and wolves and 25 yards [23 meters] away from ALL OTHER wild animals. Drive safely, keep your distance from animals, and take pictures.

You've been driving south on the Lower Grand Loop Road. Just keep driving south heading towards the Mud Volcano area.

Mud Volcano and Sulphur Caldron:

Park your car in the main Mud Volcano parking area. It will be just past the Sulphur Caldron area (on your left), but DON'T PARK in the Sulphur Caldron parking area. Just continue down the road about a hundred yards [91 meters] and the main lot will be off to your right. It's a pretty good sized lot so you shouldn't have too much trouble.

In this area there are two wonderful thermal features – Mud Volcano and Sulphur Caldron. The Mud Volcano area has a nice sized parking lot and it's usually pretty easy to find parking in this area.

Walk up onto the small mountain

or large hill – whichever way you want to look at it – and enjoy bubbling mud pots, small caldrons, Dragon's Breath, fumaroles (steam vents), and a whole array of other geo-thermal and hydro-thermal features. You'll also enjoy the aromatic odor of sulphur, thanks to Mother Nature. The aromatic aroma in this area is probably the strongest in the park. Enjoy!

When you come down the Mud Volcano hill on the boardwalk, you'll notice a small parking lot on the opposite side of the road and just a bit to the north that looks like overflow parking for the main lot. Don't be fooled! It is NOT overflow parking and many people make the mistake of thinking it is – so they take off and miss a wonderful feature of the park. Just leave your car in the main Mud Volcano parking lot and walk across the Lower Grand Loop Road – WATCH OUT FOR TRAFFIC – as people zip right through this area. After you're across the road, walk up a slight hill to your left and over to the stone wall and look down. You'll see two huge bubbling mud caldrons. This is Sulphur Caldron. Take pictures as this is a feature you'll be glad you didn't miss.

Please DO NOT take your RV (small or not) over to the parking area near Sulphur Caldron. There is limited parking there at best and an RV in this area will probably get blocked in by other vehicles. Please just walk over to Sulphur Caldron from the main parking lot at Mud Volcano. Thanks.

After you get back into your car, turn left out of the Mud Volcano parking lot and head north again on the Lower Grand Loop Road.

Tower Fall Area:

You'll continue heading straight across the main intersection at the Canyon Village area. You're now on the Upper Grand Loop Road. As you drive up the road, you'll come into the Tower Fall area from the south. Park your vehicle in the main parking lot. Sometimes this can be a challenge.

At this stop you'll want to walk out to the viewing platform for Tower Fall. It's about 100 yards [91 meters] or so from the parking area, and the trail is almost flat – just one little rise right in the middle. When you get out to the viewing platform, look to your right, and you'll see what's left of Grand Canyon of the Yellowstone. Look to your left and you'll see the waterfall. It's a ribbon style waterfall. Tower Fall is said to have many, many faces in the rock formations to the right and left of the waterfall and if you look hard enough, you'll see them. They are completely natural and are NOT man made. Take pictures.

② As you walk back to the parking lot area, there is a gift shop located here. This is just this ranger's opinion and take it if you want – it's totally up to you – but they have great ice cream in this gift shop.

🛈 🔺 In the Tower Fall area there is another first-come first-serve campground called Tower Fall Campground. This is a smaller campground that is mostly intended for tent camping or pop-up tent trailers. It's reasonably popular during the busy summer season. Reservations cannot be made and, again, this campground is a first-come first-serve campground. You have to be there to register for a campsite.

③ 📷 As you leave the Tower Fall area and drive north, you'll come across some Basalt rock columns near the side of the road (on your left). When Basalt rock cools, it forms giant columns that are six-sided and can be 40 to 50 feet [13 to 15 meters] tall or more. They look like huge crystals, only they're not, because they're not transparent – they're rock! They look really cool – no pun intended – and there are hundreds of them. As you enter this area, since they're along the side of the road, everyone will be able to see them, especially the driver. Now drivers ... don't get transfixed on them or there goes the paintjob on your car. Watch the road. Now everyone BUT the driver – look to the east (to your right) – and you'll see thousands more of these Basalt rock columns along the far side of the canyon wall of Grand Canyon of the Yellowstone. Take pictures.

Continue driving north out of the Basalt rock column area on the Upper Grand Loop Road.

Tower-Roosevelt Area:

When driving into this area, you'll see a large intersection, and the Tower-Roosevelt complex will be off to your left. You'll see stables, corrals, a restaurant, cabins, and a whole array of other amenities. Turn left into this area.

This portion of the park is a road junction named for both the Tower area of the park together with the Roosevelt connection to the park. The Tower-Roosevelt junction connects the northern end of the park with the northeast entrance and Cooke City via the Lamar Valley and the north portion of the park at Mammoth Hot Springs.

President Teddy Roosevelt did visit this area in the park in 1903 while he was here dedicating the entry arch at the north gate (more about that later). He stayed in the area but contrary to popular belief, he did NOT dine in the famous restaurant at Tower-Roosevelt junction as the lodge wasn't built until 1920. Keep in mind that back in 1903 the park was managed by the United States Army Cavalry stationed at Mammoth Hot Springs (more about that later too). Take pictures.

This area is a good spot to take a break from the car and get out and walk around a bit.

This area also has rustic cabins

and horse-drawn stagecoach rides as well as cowboy barbeques during the height of the summer visitation season. Reservations can be made through Xanterra at 307-344-7311.

When you're done at Tower-Roosevelt and back at the large intersection, drive straight across the intersection and head toward Lamar Valley.

Lamar Valley Area:

The drive through Lamar Valley from the Tower-Roosevelt junction is remarkable. The road leads from the junction to Cooke City, and if you continue toward Red Lodge, you'll pass over the Bear Tooth Pass – a very curvy road with breathtaking views back toward the park. If you're traveling in an RV any larger than about 18 feet [5.5 meters], strongly consider what you might be facing. Most of the turns are tight hairpin turns, and the altitude is about 10,000 feet [3,048 meters] plus. Spring and fall temps are low, and spring drives are nice, but huge accumulations of snow during the winter and the carved-out road from the snowplows make the view back toward the park nearly impossible. This is also a major trouble area with black ice. This pass is closed any time it snows – even sometimes in the middle of summer. Take pictures if you can (be sure to stop safely off the roadway).

⚠ The Lamar Valley has lots of WILD animals. The primary animals that roam this area are bison, elk, pronghorn, wolves and an occasional grizzly bear. Seasonally, there are sometimes moose in the area as well. You'll probably get into animal jams (traffic jams caused by animals) as visitors try and take photos of wild animals. Most times the animals are a ways away and easy to photograph. Sometimes they are right up on the roadway, and people get way too close to them for their own safety. People DO get injured when attacked. Please stay a MINIMUM of 100 yards [91 meters] from bears and wolves and 25 yards [23 meters] away from ALL OTHER wild animals. Drive safely, keep your distance from animals, and take pictures.

①📷 As you're heading eastward from the Tower-Roosevelt junction, you'll pass through an area with large boulders on the left edge of the road and just about the time when you get a first glimpse of the Lamar River, you'll be at the top of a small hill. There are turnouts to your right, and if you stop during the warmer months there is a nesting pair of

Osprey just across the river high up in the trees. They seem to be there every season. There are also nesting pairs of Eagles as well, but not seen as often as the Osprey. Take pictures.

②📷 As you continue traveling down the small hill you'll see a small sign on the right edge of the road marking the beginning of the Lamar Valley. The valley is home to several herds of bison and elk; and seasonally moose visit this area of the park. Pronghorn antelope, and wolves are present, as well as an occasional grizzly bear. Lots of other smaller animals inhabit the valley as well. Take pictures.

③📷 As you enter the furthest part of the Lamar Valley road nearing the towns of Silver Gate and Cooke City, look to your left up on top of the cliff areas for Big Horn Sheep. This is one of the areas they tend to frequent. You'll probably need binoculars and a good telephoto lens on your camera, but they're up there. Take pictures.

🛈🚻 There are no services at all in the Lamar Valley area other than gravity style restroom facilities at the road leading to Slough Creek Campground and a couple more in one of the larger turnouts toward the northeast gate on the south side of the road.

(I) (A) Within the Lamar Valley there are two campgrounds. The first is Slough Creek Campground located midway in the valley. The second is Pebble Creek Campground located further to the east toward the north-eastern gate to the park. Both are reasonably popular during the busy summer season with fishing activities. Reservations cannot be made, and these two campgrounds are both on a first-come first-serve basis. You have to be there to register for a campsite.

Drive out of the Lamar Valley the way you came in. Turn right again at that large Tower-Roosevelt intersection you saw earlier. You'll be heading west on the Upper Grand Loop Road.

Petrified Tree:

Features (I) [📷] 🚶

Petrified Tree entrance road will be on your left after you leave the Tower-Roosevelt junction. Turn left into this area.

1 [📷] The road is all of a quarter-mile long and dead ends at the Petrified Tree. Walk up the slight incline to the tree. Please respect the fence. Take pictures.

This area has been frequented by moose, especially early or late in the summer season. Watch the hill areas to the south of the Petrified Tree road for these animals. Take pictures.

When you drive out of the Petrified Tree area, turn left at the intersection with the Upper Grand Loop Road and continue to head toward Mammoth Hot Springs.

Mammoth Hot Springs:

As you enter the Mammoth Hot Springs area you'll come to an intersection. Turn left and drive towards the parking areas and park your car along the right side of the hill. RV parking at the bottom of the hill below the terraces is very limited, even for smaller RVs. The park has set aside the east side (on your left) of the road for larger vehicles, but most times cars have invaded that area too. Do the best you can when parking your RV but be ready for someone to block you in and make it a challenge to get out of there.

Located in this part of the park is Mammoth Hot Springs, a large concentration of layered terraces of super-heated water. The water contains high concentrations of Travertine in solution which, when the water crests over the edge of each pool, drops microscopic amounts of Travertine minerals at the top edge of the pool which form the pools.

There is a National Park Service Albright Visitor Center in this part of the park. During the summer visitation season there are National Park Service rangers who can help guide you to anywhere in the park you'd like to go. Just stop in and ask.

The National Park Service Visitor Center in the Mammoth area is called the Albright Visitor Center, and its main focus is all about the history of Yellowstone National Park. Take pictures.

The Mammoth area of the park is Yellowstone National Park headquarters. You'll notice a larger presence of government vehicles in this area as well as quite an array of visitor amenities.

1 The terraces are best viewed from

the lower area but that can change from season to season. Look for steam wafting up and that's your clue on which way to go. Walk up onto one of the boardwalks in this area, and you'll see the terraces right in front of you. Stay on the boardwalks, please. Serious damage can be done to the fragile terrace framework if you leave the boardwalks for any reason. Since the best viewing areas for the terraces change from year to year so it's always wise to ask at the National Park Service Visitor Center for the latest information. Take pictures.

In the fall, during the elk rut, there are usually large concentrations of elk walking about in the Mammoth Hot Springs area. Remember I mentioned to stay a minimum of 25 yards [23 meters] away from these animals. They are capable of charging you or standing on their hind legs – much like a dog would do – and swinging their front feet at you in a bicycle type motion. The hooves on the end of those two front feet are very hard and can tear you up. If there are males present – the ones with the antlers – they are very protective of their harems of females. STAY AT LEAST 25 YARDS [23 METERS] AWAY FROM ALL ANIMALS, including the elk. Park service rangers are usually around to keep people at a safe distance. Please don't get too close as we want you to leave the park with your health intact. Thanks.

Drive south out the main part of the Mammoth area and up the hill at the south end. If you have a standard sized automobile or small truck, you can drive along the Upper Terrace Drive just south of the terraces. At the top of the hill, there's an entrance (on your right) to the Upper Terrace Loop.

DO NOT go into this drive if you're towing anything, in a bus of any sort, in an RV of any length, have a dually, or are larger than a normal vehicle. You'll see a 'restriction' sign at the entrance so if you're in a large vehicle, park just outside the gate with all the tour buses, as the road is very narrow in spots and you WILL just get stuck – the tow bills, we've heard, are pretty stiff for a tow truck to get you out. Please don't drive in there in any vehicle larger than a normal one.

② You can walk on the boardwalks and get into this area from the Lower Terrace boardwalk loops as well. In a normal vehicle, you can enter the gate, stay to the right and park about a hundred yards [91 meters] or so into the drive. Walk down into an older area of Mammoth Hot Springs and see what happens after eons of Travertine minerals continually depositing themselves. The area looks somewhat like the moon. Take pictures.

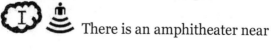 There is an amphitheater near

the campground in this area of the park. There are nightly ranger-led power point presentations about historical, natural, hydrothermal, cultural, or animal related topics in the park. The programs begin at dusk and start times vary with the season, so check at one of the visitor centers for the times. You can also check for the times in the green section in the middle of the park newspaper available when you entered the park, or you can pick one up at a visitor center.

This area is one of nine locations in the park that operate the Junior Ranger Program. There is a National Park Service Visitor Center in this area where you can purchase the Junior Ranger materials for a nominal fee. A ranger can explain how the program works to your child/children. Age range is from 4 years to 13+ years of age, but it's actually fun for the whole family. So don't let age stop you from participating in the very popular Junior Ranger program. It's great!!

Located in the Mammoth Hot Springs area is the Mammoth Hot Springs Hotel. It's one of the famous old historic structures in the park. If you're looking for historic and upscale, this is the place. Located in the heart of the Mammoth area you can walk to virtually everything worth seeing in the area. This is a very popular place to stay in the park and reservations are a must during the busy season. Reservations can be made through Xanterra at 307-344-7311.

In the vicinity of the Mammoth Hot Springs area there is a campground. It's located down the first hill from the main Mammoth Hot Springs area. This is a reasonably popular campground during the summer season. Reservations cannot be made as this campground is on a first-come first-serve basis only. You have to be there to register for a campsite.

As you leave the Upper Terraces area, you'll want to go south which, for most normal sized vehicles, is a right turn. If you parked out by the tour buses because you are in a larger than normal vehicle, just head south away from the main Mammoth Hot Springs area.

Norris Geyser Basin Area:
(You may not have time to see this area with only two days)

Cautions Ⓐ ⚠ 🚫🐕 🚭

🚗 As you head south on the Upper Grand Loop Road, you'll come across that same large 4-way stop intersection at Norris Geyser Basin area where you were earlier in this plan. Remember this intersection? Turn right into Norris Geyser Basin.

🚶 There is a National Park Service Museum and Information Station in this part of the park. During the summer visitation season there are National Park Service rangers who can help guide you to anywhere in the park you'd like to go. Just stop in and ask.

ⓘ This area is also very popular in the summer season and the parking lot becomes overloaded quite easily. If you see a road barrier up near the entrance to Norris Geyser Basin, this means law enforcement rangers are metering cars into and out of the parking lot to avoid gridlock. Just wait a short while out by the main intersection, and they'll let you in based on the number of cars exiting the area.

① 🌳 ♨ Norris Geyser Basin. This is the oldest, most dramatic, and geologically active area of the park. This geyser basin is home to the world's tallest geyser – Steamboat Geyser – that erupts on a very sporadic basis. When it does go off, it's something to behold. After the initial eruptive event which lasts only a short time, the geyser goes into a steam phase with steam blasting up about 300 feet [91 meters] for about 24 hours. There's also a walkway that goes right over a geo-thermal area, as well as loads of other geysers, hot springs, and steam vents. Take pictures.

This area is one of nine locations in the park that operate the Junior Ranger Program. There is a National Park Service Information Station in this area where you can purchase the Junior Ranger materials for a nominal fee. A ranger can explain how the program works to your child/children. Age range is from 4 years to 13+ years of age, but it's actually fun for the whole family. So don't let age stop you from participating in the very popular Junior Ranger program. It's great!!

Near the Norris Geyser Basin is the Norris Campground. It's located just north of the main junction entrance to the geyser basin. This is a reasonably popular campground during the summer season. Reservations cannot be made as this campground is on a first-come first-serve basis only. You have to be there to register for a campsite.

This is the end of this Two Day Ranger Plan. I hope you had a good time, enjoyed the park, and are excited about coming back again soon. Thank you for following this plan.

Please drive safely as you leave the park!

NOTE FROM THE AUTHOR

Please do me a huge favor. IF you like this
book and it helped you navigate your way
around Yellowstone, please, please, please ...
take a moment and let the world know
through social media such as Facebook,
Twitter, email and text messaging, and please
write a review. Thank you.

Chapter Eight

3-4 Day Ranger Plan

Since you have three to four days to see the park, now I can show you more and give you a much better sense of what Yellowstone National Park is all about: (geysers, hot springs, bubbling mud, a BIG waterfall and several other waterfalls, a nice hike or two, the terraces, and some wild animals).

Mark On Your Map

Old Faithful, Morning Glory Pool (hike), Grand Geyser, Kepler Cascades, Lone Star Geyser Hike, Grand Prismatic Spring, Firehole Lake Drive, Fountain Paint Pots, Firehole Canyon Drive, Madison Junction, Gibbon Falls, Beryl Spring, Virginia Cascades, Canyon Village Area, Hayden Valley, Mud Volcano, Sulphur Caldron, Fishing Bridge Area, Lake Butte Overlook, Lake Village Area, West Thumb Geyser Basin and Grant Village Area, Mt. Washburn Hike, Tower Fall Area, Tower-Roosevelt Area, Lamar Valley Area, Petrified Tree, Mammoth Hot Springs, Gateway Arch area, and the Upper Terraces. You may not be able to see Norris Geyser Basin Area, depending upon daylight and the amount of time you have left in your day.

Use the map guides on the next two pages.

Mark the Ranger Day Plan stops shown here onto the park map you downloaded from the internet.

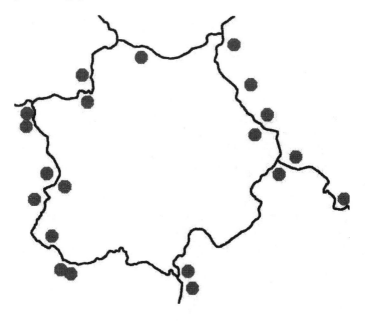

Lower Grand Loop Road

● This indicates a park feature you should highlight on a park map

3-4 Day Ranger Plan

Mark the Ranger Day Plan stops shown here onto the park map you downloaded from the internet.

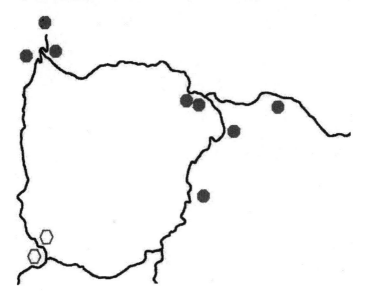

Upper Grand Loop Road

⬢ This indicates a park feature you should highlight on a park map

⬡ This indicates a park feature you MAY NOT have the time to see based upon the time you have allowed.

Old Faithful
(Upper Geyser Basin):

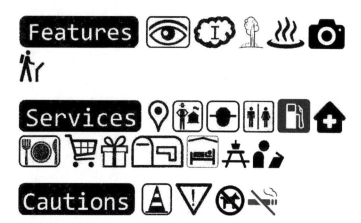

Look on the park map you highlighted, locate Old Faithful Geyser, and drive to this area. As you head south, or north, on Lower Grand Loop Road, you'll come across an exit that looks much like a freeway exit back home. Follow the sign for Old Faithful and exit to the east. Your adventure has begun!

There is a National Park Service Visitor Education Center in this part of the park. During the summer visitation season there are National Park Service rangers who can help guide you to anywhere in the park you'd like to go. Just stop in and ask.

The main focus of the Old Faithful Visitor Education Center focuses around the geology that

created Yellowstone National Park. From fumaroles, to steam vents, to geysers, to bubbling mud, to the volcano itself. Stop in and take a few minutes to wrap your mind around the catastrophic events that shaped the park.

(1) You HAVE to take in Old Faithful Geyser. Why? Because it's Old Faithful Geyser, that's why. The geyser erupts about every 96 minutes – plus or minus 10 minutes. Each geyser eruption is dependent on the previous eruption so don't expect us to give you a "schedule." This is NOT an automated process where we push a button or use a computer for each eruption. This is totally natural and dependent on the super-heated water beneath. You can stop in at any visitor center and the rangers there will be glad to give you the next eruption time. This is one of the more important things we do. Take pictures.

(2) You have enough time to walk around behind Old Faithful Geyser and look for the sign leading you up to Observation Point. You'll have to time this for about a half hour before the next eruption of the geyser. This is a short hike up onto a hill that will give you a unique view of an Old Faithful eruption. When you get up to Observation Point, sit for a while and when the eruption is near, get those cameras ready. When Old Faithful

erupts, it will erupt up to your eye level instead of erupting up and away from you, as if you were down on the viewing platform by the geyser. So you'll be even with the top of the eruption. It's a pretty neat vantage point and worth the hike up the hill. Take pictures.

You'll see that you can also continue hiking out toward Solitary Geyser. This is OK if you want to, but strongly consider having bear spray with you if you try to extend this hike on the hill any further than you have already gone. Not nearly as many people go out to Solitary Geyser as do the Observation Point hike. Just think about your safety a bit here, and consider what danger you may be in. It's up to you.

③ You have time in this Ranger Day Plan, so after you get down to the bottom of the hill again, continue walking around behind Old Faithful Geyser (stay on the trails and boardwalks) and see hundreds of other geo-thermal and hydro-thermal features behind Old Faithful up on Geyser Hill. You have time in this Ranger Day Plan and could actually spend an entire day just visiting the Old Faithful area. I encourage you to do exactly that if you want to. Take pictures.

④ Walk over to the Old Faithful Inn – the building with a bunch of flags up on top.

This is the structure that was saved from the fires of 1988 by hundreds of brave firefighters who basically put their backs to the building and any fire that was anywhere near them, they put it out. Thank you firefighters. Go into the lobby area, I'm not going to tell you where, but look for the clock. That's right ... the clock. Look around and if you can't see it, ask someone in Concierge or the gift shop where the clock is and when they show you, you'll be a bit embarrassed. It's one of those things that's right in front of your face and sometimes your eyes don't see it. Have fun with it. Take pictures.

⑤ 📷 There is a short tour of the Old Faithful Inn you can take and hear all about the building, its construction, and its history. The tours are given by Xanterra and while you're in the lobby if you go over to the railing area near the clock, you should have found earlier, you'll notice a small sign showing the times for the building tours, or check with Concierge and ask them. While you're waiting for the tour to begin, look up, and notice that the entire roof is held up by timber and wood without many supporting posts. Yet this same roof is capable of holding immense weight when snow accumulations can be very high. It's pretty amazing. Up near the peak, you also see the walkway that provides outside access to where the flags that run along the ridgeline of the Inn are raised and lowered each day. Don't look up too long though ... you'll get a neck cramp. Take pictures.

Also, at the Old Faithful Inn, there is an outdoor viewing platform area (a parking area cover) above the drop-off area for cars and buses at the front of the building by the lobby. Go into the lobby area, walk to the back-left area of the lobby, and walk up the staircase. Walk forward and out the glass doors onto the viewing area. This is a good place to take a picnic lunch, and view Old Faithful Geyser eruptions. You can bring your own packed lunch or buy prepared meals at the cafés or delicatessens in the Inn.

This area is one of nine locations in the park that operate the Junior Ranger Program. There is a National Park Service Visitor Center in this area where you can purchase the Junior Ranger materials for a nominal fee. A ranger can explain how the program works to your child/children. Age range is from 4 years to 13+ years of age, but it's actually fun for the whole family. So don't let age stop you from participating in the very popular Junior Ranger program. It's great!!

Old Faithful Inn is one of approximately 900 historic buildings in the park. It was originally built back in the early

1900s and boasts beautiful breathtaking views of Old Faithful Geyser, hundreds of geothermal and hydrothermal features, surrounding mountain areas, and is a major lodging place in this area of the park. Want to stay in a famous and historic area of the park? This is one of those places. This major hotel has it all, from upscale rooms, the finest dining, gift shops, and evening entertainment during peak season. It has a large number of rooms. Lodging here is managed by Xanterra on a reservation only basis. Xanterra can be contacted at 307-344-7311. Take pictures.

Old Faithful Lodge is available for overnight stays and features nice rooms as well as eating and dining areas. It too has a large number of rooms. Lodging here is managed by Xanterra on a reservation only basis and can be contacted at 307-344-7311.

Snow Lodge is available for overnight stays and features nice rooms as well as eating and dining areas. It has numerous rooms and is also open during the winter season as well. Lodging here is managed by Xanterra on a reservation only basis. Xanterra can be contacted at 307-344-7311. Take pictures.

There is no campground near the Old Faithful area.

Morning Glory Pool (hike):

Almost everyone has heard of Morning Glory Pool – some call it Morning Glory Spring – it's still the same place. It's located to the north of Old Faithful Geyser up near Daisy and Riverside geysers and it boasts bright green and yellow colors.

You can walk to it by following the trail toward Daisy and Riverside geysers. It's about a fifteen minute walk one way – if you don't get distracted by hundreds of other hydro-thermal features along the way. Morning Glory is about as bright as you can get with yellow and green bacterial mats reacting to sunlight. As with most other colorful hot springs, it needs good sunlight for the best photos. The best time of day is from about ten in the morning to about two or three in the afternoon as the sun is at its highest point. Take pictures.

Grand Geyser:

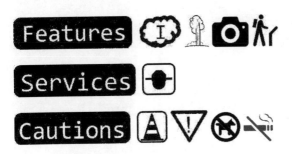

Features

Services

Cautions

1 This geyser is located behind Old Faithful in the Upper Geyser Basin. It's a very popular geyser that erupts on a somewhat regular basis. The only problem with this geyser is that it has a 5 ½ to 7 ½ hour eruption window, and then, the accuracy is plus or minus 75 minutes. This makes it somewhat difficult for the average visitor to see the eruption, simply because it's nowhere near as "faithful" as Old Faithful. But again, you have plenty of time in this Ranger Day Plan for this experience. If you happen to be in the geyser basin and Grand Geyser is about to erupt, go for it. It's called 'Grand' for a reason. It's a sizable eruption when it happens. Take pictures.

Drive out of the Old Faithful area by exiting the parking area to your right and follow the road back to the overpass area. At the overpass area, head south toward West Thumb Geyser Basin.

Kepler Cascades:

Features (I) 🌊 📷

🚗 Continue driving south on the Lower Grand Loop Road about two and a half to three miles [four to five kilometers]. If you look to the right, you'll see the sign for Kepler Cascades. Turn in here.

(I) 🌊 If you're interested in waterfalls, in Yellowstone National Park we have all three of the different types of waterfalls that exist in the world – right in the park. Kepler Cascades is one of those types as it's a "cascade" style waterfall. It's formed by multiple layers of volcanic lava that have eroded over time to form a waterfall that looks like water falling down a stairwell. So if you're interested in waterfalls, keep following what we'll call the "waterfall plan" and I'll take you to all three types.

① 🌊 Kepler Cascades is just south of Old Faithful Geyser in the Upper Geyser Basin on the Lower Grand Loop Road. This is a pretty waterfall that is right next to the edge of the road. Very easy to get to. Just park your car in the Kepler Cascades parking lot, walk about 50 feet [15 meters] out onto the viewing platform, and there it is. Take pictures.

**If you need a restroom at this point in the day, there is a restroom about three hundred feet [91 meters] away and around the corner to the south at the trailhead area for Lone Star Geyser.

NO DRIVING TIP HERE. You can just walk over to Lone Star Geyser trailhead from the Kepler Cascades parking area. In fact, there's not much parking at the trailhead for Lone Star Geyser so it's better to just leave the car at the Kepler Cascades parking area anyway. If you're not interested in the Lone Star Geyser hike, that's fine. Skip forward by driving out of the Kepler Cascades parking lot and head north (to your left) on Lower Grand Loop Road.

Lone Star Geyser (hike):

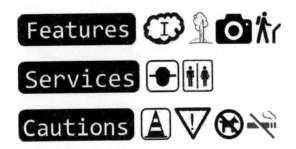

This a great little hike. It's also one of my favorite hikes in the park and you have time in this Ranger Day Plan to do this hike. The trail is almost completely flat and takes about thirty to forty minutes to get out there. The path out to the geyser is actually an old Model T Ford car road that has been changed into a biking and hiking trail. Automobiles are no longer allowed. It's about 2.4 miles [3.8 kilometers] out to the geyser so the entire hike is about 4.8 miles [7.6 kilometers]. Because the old cars didn't have much horsepower, the trail is fairly flat. And you'll be hiking through a pretty little valley with the Firehole River right next to you most of the way. This geyser is in the Old Faithful Geyser system, erupts about every 3 hours or so, and has 'major' and 'minor' eruptions.

① The first thing to do on this hike is to ask people coming back the other way on the trail if the geyser erupted and hope they say "No." This will increase your chances of seeing it erupt. The second thing to do when you arrive out at the geyser itself, is to look for a podium-like post sticking out of the ground facing the geyser. Underneath the lid of that podium is a trail log that more thoughtful hikers may have entered the last major eruption. If it last erupted at, say, 12:15 p.m. and it's now 2:55 p.m. – stick around. All you have to wait is about twenty minutes and then enjoy a fairly long eruption. Take pictures.

If you visited Kepler Cascades earlier, you can leave your car in that parking lot and just walk south around the end of the parking lot about a hundred feet [30 meters] to the trailhead for Lone Star Geyser. The parking lot at Lone Star Geyser is a doughnut style lot and has very little space for cars. By the way there is a restroom in Lone Star Geyser parking area.

🚗 When you're ready to leave the Kepler Cascades parking lot, turn left and head north on the Lower Grand Loop Road.

Grand Prismatic Spring
(Midway Geyser Basin):

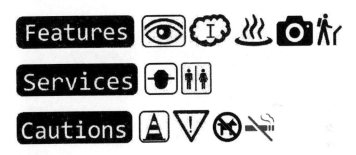

🚗 As you head north on the Lower Grand Loop Road and after you have passed under the overpass for Old Faithful, start looking to your left for the Grand Prismatic Spring parking area.

The parking lot here is grossly under-sized for the number of visitors to this area, so you'll have a challenge during peak usage times of the day getting a legal parking space. Please DO NOT park your car illegally as it may result in a parking citation. Thank you.

(1) 📷 As you walk from your car, you'll cross a bridge over the Firehole River. Stand on the bridge for a few minutes. Look up and down the river. Notice that the river is smaller upstream than it is downstream. This is because Excelsior Geyser (up the rise from where the huge water flows are entering the river) is dumping approximately 4,000 gallons [15,142 liters] of super-heated water right into the Firehole River every minute. This increases the volume of the river making it wider. It also increases the temperature of the water and there are times during the summer season when there is algae in the water north of the bridge (downstream) because of the increased temperature. Take pictures.

(2) ♨ At the top of the walkway just past the bridge is Excelsior Geyser. This very azure blue once active geyser now expels large volumes of water into the Firehole River. Please be mindful on windy days in this entire area to hold onto personal belongings such as hats, scarves, etc., as they can easily be blown right off you. It costs the park service lots of money to keep this geyser free of blown-in debris and it wrecks the uniqueness of this

place when hats, scarves, etc are in everyone's photos. Thank you. Take pictures.

③ ♨ Continue up the boardwalk where you'll come to the multi-colored Grand Prismatic Spring. This is a major attraction in the park. Again, hold onto your hats, scarves, etc. On warmer, less windy days, the steam is reduced and it's easier to see the spring itself. The opposite is true on cooler days. The steam will fog up your camera lens and eyeglasses in a heartbeat, making it a challenge to take good pictures. As with most other colorful hot springs, it needs good sunlight for the best photos so between about ten in the morning and mid-afternoon sometime are the best photo opportunities. STAY ON THE BOARDWALK AND DON'T TOUCH THE WATER!! Take pictures.

ⓘ 📷 It's common for people to want to take a photo of Grand Prismatic Spring from an elevated area. These types of photos are in many publications. The problem with this is the hillside has been unstable for years. There has been significant damage to resources and visitor safety concerns have also been an issue for quite some time. Park administration worked diligently to come up with a solution to this dilemma. In a collaborative effort between geologists, park administration, trail crews from Montana

Conservation Corps and Yellowstone Youth Conservation Corps, a new trail has been completed to an overlook with a view of Grand Prismatic Spring and the Midway Geyser Basin. The new trail is 105 feet [32 meters] high and just over one half mile long from the Fairy Falls Trail. The Fairy Falls parking area has also been redone to allow parking near the trailhead. So it's now possible to take great pictures of the spring and be safe at the same time. Please stay on this new trail to avoid further resource damage and possible fines. Thank you.

As you leave the parking lot at Grand Prismatic Spring, turn left and go north on the Lower Grand Loop Road.

Firehole Lake Drive:

As you drive north from the Grand Prismatic Spring area, you'll see the sign for Firehole

Lake Drive. Turn right IF you have a normal sized vehicle. Sorry ... NO large vehicles.

(1) After making the right turn onto Firehole Lake Drive (in your regular sized vehicle), continue on. This drive includes going past more hydro-thermal and geo-thermal features including Great Fountain Geyser, White Dome Geyser, and Firehole Lake at the back end of this loop. Great Fountain Geyser doesn't erupt very often, but when it does ... it's spectacular. Eruption times are available at any of the visitor centers in the park. Take pictures.

At the end of this one-way drive you'll find yourself just across from Fountain Paint Pots. You'll also see you can't cut across the intersection legally to enter that area. SO, turn left at this intersection and go south for a couple hundred yards [183 meters], or so, and turn right into the far end of the parking area for Fountain Paint Pots. See how easy that was?

Fountain Paint Pots
(Lower Geyser Basin):

Services 🚻 ♿

Cautions ⚠️ ⚠️ 🚫🐕 🚭

🚗 As you drive north, you'll see a sign for Fountain Paint Pots and Lower Geyser Basin. Turn left into the SOUTH end of this parking lot. Remember this entrance area as this is where you'll exit later.

ℹ️ The parking lot here is grossly under-sized for the number of visitors to this area, so you'll have a challenge during peak usage times of the day getting a legal parking space. Please DO NOT park your car illegally as it may result in a parking citation. Thanks.

①♨️ As you walk up the boardwalk you'll come to Silex Spring on your right. Take pictures.

②◉ The next thing you'll see, up and to your left, is bubbling mud at Fountain Paint Pots. If you watch very carefully and stare at the middle of the bubbling pots, you'll see one or more pots actually spit up a small ball of molten mud about the size of a quarter. It happens about every minute or two. Don't get discouraged if nothing happens, because sometimes conditions are just not right. Take pictures.

3 ♨ Walk around and take in all the hot springs, steam vents (fumaroles), and small geysers in this area. Some are below and near the lower portion of the boardwalk when standing near Fountain Paint Pots. Walk down there. Take pictures.

4 🌲 Following the upper boardwalk near the Fountain Paint Pot; walk out the boardwalk to the west and down the stairs to Clepsydra Geyser. You'll witness a fairly regular eruption of hot steam and water that ejects out the top of this geyser. Take pictures.

🚗 When you're done visiting the Fountain Paint Pot area, drive to the SOUTH end of the parking area and exit the parking area by turning left (you can't turn left at the north end of the parking area). Continue heading north on the Lower Grand Loop Road.

Firehole Canyon Drive:

Continue to drive north on Lower Grand Loop Road and you'll come upon a sign on your left for Firehole Canyon Drive. If you're in a normal size vehicle, turn left and drive in.

NO LARGE VEHICLES on Firehole Canyon Drive!! Law enforcement watches this area fairly closely.

About a quarter of a mile into this drive, you'll see the Firehole River on your right. Look around, as you're inside the volcano and it looks like it. Take pictures.

About halfway into the drive, you'll come to Firehole Falls. This is one of the more impressive waterfalls in the park. Take pictures.

Near the end of this drive, you'll come to a swimming hole set aside by the park for visitors. Enjoy yourself and cool off. BUT, be aware that this feature is not open all summer long. It's closed whenever high water or swift current become a safety issue – so check with a visitor center before getting into the water and take notice of any signage posted at the top of the stairway or elsewhere in that area. If the entrance to the stairway is blocked off – the area is CLOSED.

🚗 Also, park your car LEGALLY in this area and please don't encroach on the roadway. Keep those tires outside the white line. You can be cited for impeding traffic flow. Thank you.

ⓘ IF you decide to swim be aware there is no lifeguard on duty and swimming is at your own risk. Diving from the rocks is prohibited. Be aware that any type of flotation device is also prohibited as they sometimes get away from visitors and when they float downstream they end up tangled in the pumps of a local fish hatchery. It's expensive to repair those pumps, so please ... no floaties!!

🚗 At the end of the one-way road through Firehole Canyon, turn left at the stop sign and continue north on the Lower Grand Loop Road.

Madison Junction:

Right after you drive down a small hill and cross a bridge over the Gibbon River, you'll climb the small hill on the opposite side. Near the top of that hill is the turnoff for Madison Junction. Turn left.

Madison Junction is named for the confluence of the Firehole and Gibbon Rivers that join to become the Madison River. This is a world class fly fishing area. The Firehole River comes from the southern portion of the park – where a large concentration of geysers and hydro-thermal features are – and it winds its way northward to the Madison Junction. The Gibbon River comes from the central portion of the park before it arrives at the Madison Junction. When the two rivers meet, they become the Madison River, also known as the Madison Junction. It's the meeting of the two rivers that is the "junction," NOT the road junction. The Madison Junction area is also home to the "campfire myth" said to have taken place here. Ask any ranger and they should be able to share with you the background of the "campfire myth." As a ranger, take it from me, it's pretty interesting. Take pictures.

There is a National Park Service Information Station in this part of the park. During the summer visitation season there are National Park Service rangers who can help guide you to anywhere in the park you'd like to go. Just stop in and ask.

① 📷 While you're at the Madison Junction area, look westward down the canyon toward the town of West Yellowstone. Notice on your left (south) the mountain vegetation – mostly Lodgepole Pine trees – is generally non-existent, yet on the right (north) the trees flourish. You're standing at one of several areas in the park where you can see the aftermath of the fires of 1988 that destroyed about one third of the park. The park is just about 2.2 million acres, and the fires of 1988 consumed about 800,000 acres. Looking to your left again, further down the mountain and even with the bottom of the valley floor, you'll notice fairly large Lodgepole Pine trees here, yet this was a burn area. How can that be? Well, the trees down low are the babies of the burned trees and are being fed a constant diet of nutrients from the Gibbon and Firehole Rivers, but the trees up on the slope of the edge of the volcano – again on the left side of the valley – are barely surviving and are much less tall because of lack of nutrients. This demonstrates the stark difference between having good nutrients in the soil and not – all because of the fire of 1988. Fires in the park actually help the ecosystem.

ⓘ 📶 There is an amphitheater near the campground and the Information Station in this area of the park. There are nightly ranger-led power point presentations about historical, natural, hydrothermal, cultural, or animal related topics in the park. The programs begin at dusk and start times vary with the season, so check at one of the visitor centers for the times. You can also check for the times in the green section in the middle of the park newspaper available when you entered the park, or you can pick one up at a visitor center.

This area is one of nine locations in the park that operate the Junior Ranger Program. There is a National Park Service Information Station in this area where you can purchase the Junior Ranger materials for a nominal fee. A ranger can explain how the program works to your child/children. Age range is from 4 years to 13+ years of age, but it's actually fun for the whole family. So don't let age stop you from participating in the very popular Junior Ranger program. It's great!!

In the Madison Junction area of the park there is Madison Campground. This particular campground has some spaces large enough for smaller RVs, but is mostly sized for tent and tent trailer camping. The campground is just adjacent to the Madison Junction parking lot and is located just west of the intersection heading toward the town of

West Yellowstone. Reservations can be made through Xanterra at 307-344-7311.

When done at the Madison Junction area, get in your car and turn left when leaving the parking lot. You'll go past the road junction that heads back to the town of West Yellowstone (don't turn here) and continue north on the Lower Grand Loop Road.

Gibbon Falls:

About six miles [9.5 kilometers] north of Madison Junction, you'll come to Gibbon Falls on the east side of the road. Turn right into the parking area.

This is a pretty waterfall and a nice place to stretch your legs. It is also one of those areas that if you have an animal that needs to be walked, you can do so if you're never any further than 100 feet [30 meters] from a developed area. Be mindful of the distance though. Some people do go all the way down to the far end of the walkway to get a great picture, but are well past the 100 feet [30 meters] maximum distance from the parking lot. Please pick up after your animal. It's also an area rangers like to rove around quite a bit more than some other areas and answer visitors' questions about the park. From this area, looking to the south along the ridges of the mountains, you can also see the remnants of the last volcanic eruption 640,000 years ago. Take pictures.

If you need a restroom in this area of the park, there is no restroom right at Gibbon Falls. But just to the north up the road about a quarter mile on your left is Iron Spring picnic area, and there is a restroom at this picnic area.

From the Gibbon Falls area, turn right out of the parking lot back onto the Lower Grand Loop Road and head north again.

Beryl Spring:

Cautions ⚠️ 🚭

🚗 Beryl Spring is right along the roadway on the left side of the road, a few miles north of Gibbon Falls. You'll probably see the steam before you see the bridge or the spring. Pull off to the left side of the roadway and park your car.

ⓘ The spring is just adjacent to the Gibbon River. The spring drains into the river and produces quite a bit of steam, even on moderately warm summer days. There is a short bridge right next to the spring, which can make the drive over the bridge with a vehicle a challenge because of the 'London fog' amounts of steam wafting right over the roadway on the bridge. The spring is on your left.

① ♨️ This is a short stop. Walk a couple of hundred feet [61 meters] up near the bridge, and enjoy one of Yellowstone's lesser viewed springs but a nice one just the same. Take pictures.

🚗 From the Beryl Spring area, continue to drive north to the Norris Geyser Basin intersection. Turn right at this large 4-way stop intersection and head east towards Canyon Village. Don't worry about Norris Geyser Basin right now as we'll come back to this area later on.

Virginia Cascades:

 About five or six miles [9.5 kilometers] down the road from the Norris Geyser Basin intersection, you'll see a sign for Virginia Cascades Drive. With your normal sized vehicle, bear to the right (it's a slight "Y" intersection) onto the two mile, or so, one-way cascades drive.

This one-way road is a great little side jaunt but NO LARGE VEHICLES! If you're in a large vehicle just keep heading east toward Canyon Village. Please don't go in Virginia Cascades.

This short little road takes you past one of the "cascade" style waterfalls in the park formed by multiple layers of lava flows thousands of years ago that created small shelves of volcanic rock that the Gibbon River runs over. It's like water running down a stairwell. This creates the effect referred to as a cascade. Take pictures.

When you're done at Virginia Cascades and at

the end of the one-way drive, turn right to get back onto the Grand Loop Road and head east towards Canyon Village.

Canyon Village Area:

As you're coming into the Canyon Village area, turn right at the large 4-way stop intersection and drive south toward Fishing Bridge on the Lower Grand Loop Road.

There is a National Park Service Visitor Education Center in this part of the park. During the summer visitation season there are National Park Service rangers who can help guide you to anywhere in the park you'd like to go. Just stop in and ask.

The Canyon Village Visitor Education Center's main focus is all about the volcano. From the first eruption about 2.1 million years ago to the last eruption 640,000 years ago, this educational experience takes you all the way through. This is powerful. Take pictures.

Located in the Canyon Village area is the largest waterfall in the 'front country' area of the park. It's called Lower Falls and can be viewed best from Artist Point. The waterfall is 308 feet high, or 94 meters, and at its peak the average flow of the Yellowstone River is around 63,500 gallons per second, or for you metrically challenged folks, that's more than 240,000 liters per second. At some parts of the season the flow is much higher IF there has been an unusually high snowfall the previous winter.

The third left turn is called South Rim Drive with a sign saying "Artist Point." The parking lot for Artist Point – all the way at the end of this drive – is pretty good sized for automobiles and small RVs. Be careful if you're in a larger RV as there is limited parking for larger vehicles like RVs and tour buses. This lot also fills to capacity during the busy summer months.

After parking in the main lot walk to the east a couple of hundred yards [183 meters] over to the Lower Falls viewing platform which has a lower and upper viewing area to take pictures. This area IS handicap accessible. Take pictures.

Don't stand on the stone walls as it's

unsafe, a LONG way down, and probably not survivable.

(I) 📷 While at Artist Point you have a wonderful and dramatic view of Grand Canyon of the Yellowstone. At the viewing area between the waterfall and where you're standing is the start of the "grand canyon." If you walk around to the back side of the viewing area, you can see more of the canyon as it continues downstream. Take pictures.

🚗 On your way back from Artist Point, you could stop at Uncle Tom's Trail and take the trail down to a great view of Lower Falls. There's also a nice view of Upper Falls without taking Uncle Tom's Trail.

(2) 🌊 🚶 This hike is pretty challenging and includes trails, metal walkways, and an expanded metal staircase attached to the side of a huge boulder with loads of steps. It's about 500 feet [152 meters] down and about 328 steps. If you're uneasy about this, ask others coming back up what it was like, and make a decision from there. The view, though, is worth it because down on the viewing platform you'll find yourself about halfway down the full height of Lower Falls looking right at the falls itself. Now be aware there are times of the year this walkway is closed as the mist coming off the falls is too much for safe passage. The metal stairways can become slick

and can also freeze. Take pictures.

3 While you're in the same Uncle Tom's Trail parking lot, stroll over to the viewpoint of the Upper Falls – it's about a hundred feet [30 meters], or so, off to the left. Upper Falls and Lower Falls are both along the Yellowstone River. So the same 63,500 gallons [240,000 liters] of water per second flows over both waterfalls. The view is amazing. Upper Falls is 109 feet high, or about 33 meters. Take pictures.

Turn right out of the Uncle Tom's parking lot and return back to the main Lower Grand Loop Road. Turn right and drive to the next right turn. This is Brink of the Upper Falls.

4 There is a short hike down to the top of the falls that has a pretty nice view. The hike is about 60 feet [18 meters] down and about a hundred yards [91 meters] long. When you get to the brink area look upstream. You'll notice a particularly unusual site. As the river comes down through the canyon it zigzags back and forth, and each time it turns there is a bluff hiding the turn of the water. This is because eons of water erosion changed the course of the river. The erosion and the 'turn' of the river hidden behind the bluff creates the unusual effect of making it appear that the river is colliding with itself as it zig-zags its way down the canyon before making the final turn right in front of you, then over the brink. Take pictures.

Drive back to the main loop road again and turn right. This will take you north again toward Canyon Village area. Turn right where the sign says "North Rim Drive" and "Brink of the Lower Falls." You'll see a parking lot right away, and this is where you should try to park. This parking lot fills to capacity quite often so do the best you can.

Lower Falls is the tallest waterfall in Yellowstone Park in the front country at 308 feet [94 meters] high and, again, about 63,500 gallons [240,000 liters] of water per second go over the top.

The walkway is near the start of this parking lot on the south side. The hike down to Brink of the Lower Falls can be challenging. It's about 250 to 300 feet [76 to 91 meters] down and the trail is a switchback style trail. But remember, you're at almost 8,000 feet [2,413 meters] elevation. Stand at the top of the trail and decide if you can make the journey. It's well worth it IF you can do it. Ask others that are coming back up how hard it was for them and make your decision from there. If you decide to go down, you'll be standing at the very top of the waterfall with all that water rushing right past you before it falls over the brink. It's pretty impressive. Take pictures.

Back in your car, continue to drive along North Rim Drive as it's a one-way road anyway. There are "Lookout Point" and "Grand View" viewing areas with good photo opportunities of Grand Canyon of the Yellowstone along the way. Why not stop as you can always delete the picture(s) later if you don't want them, right? As you continue along North Rim Drive, you'll also see the sign on your right for "Inspiration Point." Make the right turn and drive out to the parking lot at the end.

6 Inspiration Point is another fantastic view up and down Grand Canyon of the Yellowstone. The Minnetaree Indians called the area "Mi tse a-da-zi," which means "Rock Yellow River." Yellowstone's version of the Grand Canyon in Arizona, is called Grand Canyon of the Yellowstone and is about 22 miles [35 kilometers] long and follows the Yellowstone River up to Tower Fall area, which we'll talk about later on. Take pictures.

Drive your car back out the way you came in. Turn right (you can't turn left as the road is one-way) and continue to follow North Rim Drive. The one-way road will take you back to the Canyon Village area where the National Park Service Visitor Center for the Canyon Village area of the park is located, as well as food, restrooms, gift shops, a post office, and the lodges. Most of these facilities will be on your left as you enter the area. This area IS handicap accessible. The gas station, campground, and amphitheater will be on your right.

(I) You may be wondering why I have you back-tracking. This is because if you get to Lower Falls too late in the day, your picture quality will go way down as the sun would be getting too close to the horizon and foul up your photos. Please forgive me.

(I) If you've been following along the plan so far, you've now seen two "cascade" style waterfalls at Kepler Cascades and Virginia Cascades, and two "regular" waterfalls at Lower and Upper Falls. Keep going, you're doing great!

(I) There is an amphitheater near the campground in this area of the park. There are nightly ranger-led power point presentations about historical, natural, hydrothermal, cultural, or animal related topics in the park. The programs begin at dusk and start times vary with the season, so check at one of the visitor centers for the times. You can also check for the times in the green section in the middle of the park newspaper available when you entered the park, or you can pick one up at a visitor center.

This area has one of nine locations in the park that operate the Junior Ranger Program. There is a National Park Service Visitor Center in Canyon Village where you can purchase the Junior Ranger materials for a nominal fee. A ranger can explain how the program works to your child/children. Age range is from 4 years to 13+ years of age, but it's actually fun for the whole family. So don't let age stop you from participating in the very popular Junior Ranger program. It's great!!

The Canyon Village area has plenty of lodging available at Canyon Lodge but during the summer season everything is booked solid so if you want to stay in this part of the park you'll have to book early. Canyon Lodge just completed a major addition of hundreds of rooms that are brand new. This is a very popular place to stay in the park and reservations are a must during the busy season. Reservations can be made through Xanterra at 307-344-7311.

Canyon Village also has a nice campground complex. The campground here is located north of the main intersection near the gas station. Like Madison Campground, it too can handle some smaller RVs but is designed mostly for tent and tent trailer camping. Reservations can be made through

Xanterra at 307-344-7311.

🚗 When you're done in the Canyon Village area, drive back out to that large 4-way stop intersection again and turn left. You'll be heading south on the Lower Grand Loop Road.

Hayden Valley:

🚗 Continue heading south from the Canyon Village area on the Lower Grand Loop Road. After going about three or four miles [six kilometers], you'll be entering the Hayden Valley area.

💭 Hayden Valley is named for Ferdinand Vandeveer Hayden who in 1871 led one of first surveys of Yellowstone National Park and the surrounding area. Hayden was a geologist and was federally funded to document the area for possible legislation to create the park.

 Hayden Valley has lots of

WILD animals. The primary animals that roam this area are bison, elk, wolves and an occasional grizzly bear. Seasonally, there are sometimes black bear and moose in the area as well. You'll probably get into animal jams (traffic jams caused by animals) as visitors take photos of wild animals. Watch the car in front of you! Most times the animals are a ways away and easy to photograph. Sometimes they're right up on the roadway and people get WAY TOO CLOSE to them for their own safety. People DO get injured when attacked. Please stay a MINIMUM of 100 yards [91 meters] from bears and wolves and 25 yards [23 meters] away from ALL OTHER wild animals. Drive safely, keep your distance from animals, and take pictures.

You've been driving south on the Lower Grand Loop Road. Just keep driving south heading towards the Mud Volcano area.

Mud Volcano and Sulphur Caldron:

Park your car in the main Mud Volcano parking area. It will be just past the Sulphur Caldron area (on your left), but DON'T PARK in the Sulphur Caldron parking area. Just continue down the road about a hundred yards [91 meters] and the main lot will be off to your right. It's a pretty good sized lot so you shouldn't have too much trouble.

In this area there are two wonderful thermal features – Mud Volcano and Sulphur Caldron. The Mud Volcano area has a nice sized parking lot and it's usually pretty easy to find parking in this area.

1 Walk up onto the small mountain or large hill – whichever way you want to look at it – and enjoy bubbling mud pots, small caldrons, Dragon's Breath, fumaroles (steam vents), and a whole array of other geo-thermal and hydro-thermal features. You'll also enjoy the aromatic odor of sulphur, thanks to Mother Nature. The aromatic aroma in this area is probably the strongest in the park. Enjoy!

2 When you come down the Mud Volcano hill on the boardwalk, you'll notice a small parking lot on the opposite side of the road and just a bit to the north that looks like overflow parking for the main lot. Don't be fooled! It is NOT overflow parking and many people make the mistake of thinking it is – so they take off and miss a wonderful feature of the park. Just leave your car in the main Mud Volcano parking lot and walk across the Lower Grand Loop Road – WATCH OUT FOR TRAFFIC – as people zip right through this area. After you're across the road, walk up a slight hill to your left and over to the stone wall and look down. You'll see two huge bubbling mud caldrons. This is Sulphur Caldron. Take pictures as this is a feature you'll be glad you didn't miss.

Please DO NOT take your RV (small or not) over to the parking area near Sulphur Caldron. There is limited parking there at best and an RV in this area will probably get blocked in by other vehicles. Please just walk over to Sulphur Caldron from the main parking lot at Mud Volcano. Thanks.

After you get back into your car, turn right out of the Mud Volcano parking lot and head south on the Lower Grand Loop Road toward Fishing Bridge.

Fishing Bridge Area:

🚗 Watch for the sign for the Fishing Bridge area. The turn into the Fishing Bridge area is a left turn.

👤 There is a National Park Service Museum and Visitor Center in this part of the park. During the summer visitation season there are National Park Service rangers who can help guide you to anywhere in the park you'd like to go. Just stop in and ask.

ℹ️ The Fishing Bridge Museum and Visitor Center's main focus is on fishing and the history in this area of the park. It's very interesting and informative. Fishing Bridge itself is an old historic bridge that in the not-too-distant past allowed fishing right from the bridge (hence the name). There are native Cutthroat Trout swimming in and out of the lake and into the Yellowstone River constantly. It WAS a great place to fish – BUT – too many issues with traffic congestion, tangled fishing lines, and upset visitors have changed all of that. Fishing Bridge is now CLOSED to fishing of any kind. Please obey the signs. Thanks. Take pictures.

ℹ️ There is an amphitheater near the visitor center in this area of the park. There are nightly ranger-led power point presentations about historical, natural, hydrothermal, cultural, or animal related topics in the park. The programs begin at dusk and start times vary with the season, so check at one of the visitor centers for the times. You can also check for the times in the green section in the middle of the park newspaper available when you entered the park, or you can pick one up at a visitor center.

This area has one of nine locations in the park that operate the Junior Ranger Program. There is a National Park Service Visitor Center in Fishing Bridge where you can purchase the Junior Ranger materials for a nominal fee. A ranger can explain how the program works to your child/children. Age range is from 4 years to 13+ years of age, but it's actually fun for the whole family. So don't let age stop you from participating in the very popular Junior Ranger program. It's great!!

There are showers and laundry facilities in this area of the park.

If you need postal service or medical clinic facilities you'll have to make the short drive over to the Lake Village area for these services.

The Fishing Bridge Campground is the only one like it in the entire park. This campground is set up for hard-sided recreational vehicles ONLY. There are no tent spaces in this campground. It's also very popular during the summer season. Reservations can be made through Xanterra at 307-344-7311.

① 🚶‍♂️ Just east of the main Fishing Bridge area is a short kid-friendly hike out to Storm Point. Look for the small parking area for Indian Pond (on your right when going to the east). When you walk out to the point, if it's a nice warm day, keep an eye out for Marmots – there are hundreds of them. The warm summer days bring them out for some much needed vitamin D (just kidding – they probably just want to warm up a bit). The kids usually get a kick out of seeing them. Please don't feed them though as we don't want them to become aggressive looking for 'human food' from visitors who come there in the future. Thanks.

📷 Also out at the end of the Storm Point trail is a great opportunity for a very nice picture of Yellowstone Lake. The sun rises and sets away from the direction you're taking your shot – you'd be pointing your camera/cell phone toward the south – so you won't get any reflection from the sun in your photo. If it's a clear day the Grand Teton Mountains will be in the background. Take pictures.

② 🚶‍♂️ Also as you wind your way back around to the west, you'll follow the trail into a wooded area. This is a nice, quiet, peaceful little walk of about a quarter-mile which opens up at the end to a small meadow and the trail then comes back on itself to the main trail you walked out on originally. Take pictures.

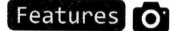 From the Storm Point area if you're in a normal size vehicle head east toward the east entry gate and Cody, Wyoming. If you're in a LARGE VEHICLE, please just head back towards the Fishing Bridge area.

Lake Butte Overlook:

 As you drive east on the east entrance road towards Cody, Wyoming, you'll see the sign for Lake Butte Overlook. Turn left and drive up the hill. NO LARGE VEHICLES are allowed as the grade is too great. If you're in a large vehicle, please don't try this hill. Thanks.

This is a great place for scenic views of the park. At the top of Lake Butte Overlook looking to the south – on a clear day

– you'll have Yellowstone Lake in the foreground, the park's Red Mountain range in the mid-ground, and the Grand Tetons in the background of any photos you take. It's a real nice place to have a picnic lunch and enjoy the views. Dress in layers though, as it gets pretty breezy up there, and sometimes the temperature is much cooler than down below. Take pictures.

At the bottom of the hill at Lake Butte Overlook, you'll need to turn to the right and head back toward the Fishing Bridge area. When you arrive at the intersection with the Lower Grand Loop Road just west of the bridge itself, turn left and head south again.

Lake Village Area:

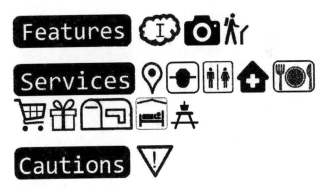

As you drive south on the Lower Grand Loop

Road, the sign for Lake Village is about three miles [4.8 kilometers] south of the turn you just made. Turn left into the Lake Village area.

(1) 🛏 The Lake Hotel is one of the famous historic buildings in the park. It was originally built back in the early 1900s and is the site of motion pictures, beautiful breathtaking views of the lake and surrounding mountains, and is a major lodging area in the park. Want to stay in a historic area of the park? This is one of those places. This major hotel has it all, from upscale rooms, the finest dining, gift shops, and evening entertainment during peak season. It has a large number of rooms available during the summer season, and is NOT open during the winter season. Lodging here is managed by Xanterra on a reservation only basis. Xanterra can be contacted at 307-344-7311. Take pictures.

(2) 🛏 Lake Lodge is also one of the famous historic buildings in the park. It, too, has beautiful breathtaking views of the lake and surrounding mountains, and is a major lodging area in this part of the park. This is also one of those 'must see' places. Lodging here is also managed by Xanterra on a reservation only basis. Xanterra can be contacted at 307-344-7311. Take pictures.

Lake Hotel and Lake Lodge both have dining rooms and are very nice places to dine. Both structures are historic. Upscale menus, great views, and ambiance await you. Reservations are managed by Xanterra and can be made via phone at 307-344-7311. Take pictures.

There are also cabins for rent during the peak summer season in this area of the park. Reservations are managed by Xanterra and can be made via phone at 307-344-7311.

If you need fuel, there is a gas station in the area but you'll have to make the short drive over to the Fishing Bridge area for this service.

As you leave the Lake Village area, turn left again and head south on the Lower Grand Loop Road.

West Thumb Geyser Basin and Grant Village:

As you drive south on the Lower Grand Loop Road, watch for the signs leading you into the West Thumb Geyser Basin.

There is a National Park Service Visitor Center in this part of the park at Grant Village. There is also a National Park Service Information Station in the West Thumb Geyser Basin. During the summer visitation season there are National Park Service rangers who can help guide you to anywhere in the park you'd like to go. Just stop in and ask.

West Thumb Geyser Basin. This is home to the most recent volcanic activity in the park, which was a huge lava flow about 70,000 years ago preceded by earlier lava flows about 174,000 years ago. The geyser basin has several hot springs and steam vents along with other great features to look at. Take pictures.

1 Fishing Cone Geyser is located in West Thumb Geyser Basin near the bottom edge of the boardwalk just off the shore into Yellowstone Lake. There is a photo taken about a hundred years ago and a short story of a guy standing on top of the geyser – you are

NOT allowed to do this today – and he's fishing. So, as the story goes he catches a fish, dunks it in the geyser – which does what? That's right ... dunking the fish into the geyser cooks the fish. He then tosses out another baited line, and while he's waiting to catch the next fish, he can eat the one he just caught. Check out the picture and story in front of this feature. Take pictures.

2 Drive along Yellowstone Lake for beautiful views of this stunning alpine lake. This lake is the largest lake in North America above 7,000 feet [2,134 meters] elevation, making it an alpine lake. Feel free to stop at one of the many turnouts in this area (please keep all four wheels of your vehicle outside the white line at the edge of the roadway or you could be subject to a citation for impeding traffic flow), take your shoes off, and enjoy a rather brisk dip in the lake. Warning: depending upon the time of year, this is a very cold lake and getting in further than your knees is not recommended as hypothermia can easily set in. Take pictures.

I There is an amphitheater near the campground and the Grant Village Visitor Center in this area of the park. There are nightly ranger-led power point presentations about historical, natural, hydrothermal, cultural, or animal related topics in the park.

The programs begin at dusk and start times vary with the season, so check at one of the visitor centers for the times. You can also check for the times in the green section in the middle of the park newspaper available when you entered the park, or you can pick one up at a visitor center.

This area has two of nine locations in the park that operate the Junior Ranger Program. There is a National Park Service Visitor Center in Grant Village and an Information Station in West Thumb where you can purchase the Junior Ranger materials for a nominal fee. A ranger can explain how the program works to your child/children. Age range is from 4 years to 13+ years of age, but it's actually fun for the whole family. So don't let age stop you from participating in the very popular Junior Ranger program. It's great!!

There are showers and laundry facilities in this area of the park.

The Grant Village area of the park has a campground and can handle a few smaller RVs but is mostly intended for tent camping or tent trailers. This is a popular campground during the busy summer season. Reservations can be made through Xanterra at 307-344-7311.

There is another campground in the vicinity of Grant Village. It's called Lewis Lake and is south of the Grant Village area. This is a smaller campground that is mostly intended for tent camping or pop-up tent trailers. It's also one of the last to fill up during the busy summer season. Reservations cannot be made, and this campground is a first-come first-serve campground. You have to be there to register for a campsite.

When you're done exploring the West Thumb and Grant Village areas of the park, head north again on the Lower Grand Loop Road back toward Fishing Bridge. Most times that's a right hand turn. You're going to be driving quite a ways. You'll go past both the Fishing Bridge area as well as the Canyon Village area. You'll continue heading straight across the main 4-way stop intersection at the Canyon Village area. You're now on the Upper Grand Loop Road. Keep going.

Mt. Washburn Hike:

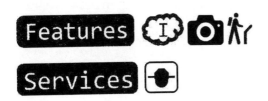

Cautions ⚠ 🚭

About five or six miles [9.5 kilometers] up the road, you'll come to the Dunraven Pass summit. There is a parking lot on the right for the Mt. Washburn hike. This parking lot is under-sized and is full quite often during the busy summer season. Another parking area is at Chittenden Road, about four miles [6.5 kilometers] north of this parking area, right on the inside of a hairpin turn.

Mt. Washburn is one of the great hikes in Yellowstone National Park. You have a superb view from the top of the mountain, and if you have the physical ability to climb the mountain on a clear day you'll be richly rewarded with a southern view of Yellowstone National Park, which also includes the Grand Teton peaks in the distance, as well as being able to see the curvature of the earth. It's pretty spectacular. This location is also a park fire ranger lookout location. The building at the top is three stories with the top story looking like an airport control tower so the ranger has a 360 degree view of the park. After all, he's up there to watch for fires. The second floor is the residence area and the lower floor is for public viewing and is a great place for a picnic meal while enclosed in a glass room.

① 🚶 There are two ways to hike up to the top. From the Dunraven Pass parking lot, there is a trail that's about 6 miles [9.5

kilometers] roundtrip to the top of Mt. Washburn with stunning views on the way up. This trail is the more popular of the two. The second trail to the top of Mt. Washburn is from the next turnoff up the road to your right called Chittenden Road. Drive up Chittenden Road – a dirt road – to the top and park in the dirt parking lot. From the south end of the parking lot is the service road the park uses to get to the top of the mountain. This hike is a bit steeper than the Dunraven trail but it's only 4.2 miles [6.8 kilometers] long roundtrip. The difference in the two trails – setting aside that one is a service road – is that the trip up from the Chittenden Road side isn't as stunning as the Dunraven side because you're just hiking up a service road and most of the view is just going up the road. Maybe that's why the Dunraven trail is preferred by most. Take LOTS of pictures. (As a side note – if you're a bicyclist, you can bicycle up the service road from the Chittenden end to the top if you want to.)

The temperatures at the top of Mt. Washburn can be pretty cold. Brutally cold sometimes. It's also quite windy at the top, so when the cold temperatures and the wind combine, it can make the hike memorable for you for all the wrong reasons. Dress in layers and be ready for some very cold temperatures.

🚗 When you get back to your car in either parking lot, go to the entrance to the parking area, turn right, and continue to drive north on Upper Grand Loop Road.

Tower Fall Area:

🚗 As you continue driving, you'll come into the Tower Fall area from the south. Park your vehicle in the main parking lot. Sometimes this can be a challenge.

① At this stop you'll want to walk out to the viewing platform for Tower Fall. It's about 100 yards [91 meters] or so from the parking area, and the trail is almost flat – just one little rise right in the middle. When you get out to the viewing platform, look to your right, and you'll see what's left of Grand Canyon of the Yellowstone. Look to your left and you'll see the waterfall. It's a ribbon style waterfall. Tower Fall is said to have many, many faces in the rock formations to the right and left of the waterfall and if you look hard enough, you'll see them. They are completely natural and are NOT man made. If you've been following the "waterfall plan", this ribbon style waterfall at Tower Fall is the last of the three waterfalls in the plan. Take pictures.

② As you walk back to the parking lot area, there is a gift shop located here. This is just this ranger's opinion and take it if you want – it's totally up to you – but they have great ice cream in this gift shop.

In the Tower Fall area there is another first-come first-serve campground called Tower Fall Campground. This is a smaller campground that is mostly intended for tent camping or pop-up tent trailers. It's reasonably popular during the busy summer season. Reservations cannot be made and, again, this campground is a first-come first-serve campground. You have to be there to register for a campsite.

③ As you leave the Tower Fall area and drive north, you'll come across some Basalt rock columns near the side of the road (on your left). When Basalt rock cools, it forms giant columns that are six-sided and can be 40 to 50 feet [13 to 15 meters] tall or more. They look like huge crystals, only they're not, because they're not transparent – they're rock! They look really cool – no pun intended – and there are hundreds of them. As you enter this area, since they're along the side of the road, everyone will be able to see them, especially the driver. Now drivers ... don't get transfixed on them or there goes the paintjob on your car. Watch the road. Now everyone BUT the driver – look to the east (to your right) – and you'll see thousands more of these Basalt rock columns along the far side of the canyon wall of Grand Canyon of the Yellowstone. Take pictures.

Continue driving north out of the Basalt rock column area.

Tower-Roosevelt Area:

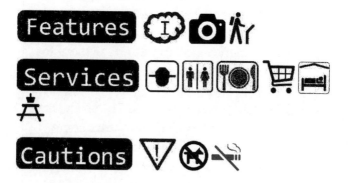

🚗 When driving into this area, you'll see a large intersection, and the Tower-Roosevelt complex will be off to your left. You'll see stables, corrals, a restaurant, cabins, and a whole array of other amenities. Turn left into this area.

ℹ️ This portion of the park is a road junction named for both the Tower area of the park together with the Roosevelt connection to the park. The Tower-Roosevelt junction connects the northern end of the park with the northeast entrance and Cooke City via the Lamar Valley and the north portion of the park at Mammoth Hot Springs.

①📷 President Teddy Roosevelt did visit this area in the park in 1903 while he was here dedicating the entry arch at the north gate (more about that later). He stayed in the area but contrary to popular belief, he did NOT dine in the famous restaurant at Tower-Roosevelt junction as the lodge wasn't built until 1920. Keep in mind that back in 1903 the park was managed by the United States Army Cavalry stationed at Mammoth Hot Springs (more about that later too). Take pictures.

② This area is a good spot to take a break from the car and get out and walk around a bit.

 This area also has rustic cabins

and horse-drawn stagecoach rides as well as cowboy barbeques during the height of the summer visitation season. Reservations can be made through Xanterra at 307-344-7311.

When you're done at Tower-Roosevelt and back at the large intersection, drive straight across the intersection and head toward Lamar Valley.

Lamar Valley Area:

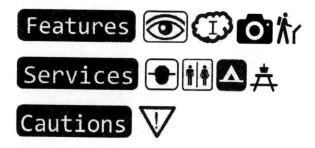

The drive through Lamar Valley from the Tower-Roosevelt junction is remarkable. The road leads from the junction to Cooke City, and if you continue toward Red Lodge, you'll pass over the Bear Tooth Pass – a very curvy road with breathtaking views back toward the park. If you're traveling in an RV any larger than about 18 feet [5.5 meters], strongly consider what you might be facing. Most of the turns are tight hairpin turns, and the altitude is about 10,000 feet [3,048 meters] plus. Spring and fall temps are low, and spring drives are nice, but huge accumulations of snow during the winter and the carved-out road from the snowplows make the view back toward the park nearly impossible. This is also a major trouble area with black ice. This pass is closed any time it snows – even sometimes in the middle of summer. Take pictures if you can (be sure to stop safely off the roadway).

The Lamar Valley has lots of WILD animals. The primary animals that roam this area are bison, elk, pronghorn, wolves and an occasional grizzly bear. Seasonally, there are sometimes moose in the area as well. You'll probably get into animal jams (traffic jams caused by animals) as visitors try and take photos of wild animals. Most times the animals are a ways away and easy to photograph. Sometimes they are right up on the roadway, and people get way too close to them for their own safety. People DO get injured when attacked. Please stay a MINIMUM of 100 yards [91 meters] from bears and wolves and 25 yards [23 meters] away from ALL OTHER wild animals. Drive safely, keep your distance from animals, and take pictures.

As you're heading eastward from the Tower-Roosevelt junction, you'll pass through an area with large boulders on the left edge of the road and just about the time when you get a first glimpse of the Lamar River, you'll be at the top of a small hill. There are turnouts to your right, and if you stop during the warmer months there is a nesting pair of

Osprey just across the river high up in the trees. They seem to be there every season. There are also nesting pairs of Eagles as well, but not seen as often as the Osprey. Take pictures.

②📷 As you continue traveling down the small hill you'll see a small sign on the right edge of the road marking the beginning of the Lamar Valley. The valley is home to several herds of bison and elk, and seasonally moose visit this area of the park. Pronghorn antelope and wolves are present; as well as an occasional grizzly bear. Lots of other smaller animals inhabit the valley as well. Take pictures.

③📷 As you travel out through the valley, on your left (north side of the road) is Buffalo Ranch. This is where the bison of Yellowstone National Park were revived after they were almost wiped out in the early 1900s. This area is now a conservation post and an area where the Yellowstone conference center is. There are also classes on all sorts of nature driven programs. Check the course descriptions and take a class, if you have the time. Information is in the park newsletter. Take pictures if you like.

④📷 As you enter the furthest part of the Lamar Valley road nearing the towns of

Silver Gate and Cooke City, look to your left up on top of the cliff areas for Big Horn Sheep. This is one of the areas they tend to frequent. You'll probably need binoculars and a good telephoto lens on your camera, but they're up there. Take pictures.

There are no services at all in the Lamar Valley area other than gravity style restroom facilities at the road leading to Slough Creek Campground and a couple more in one of the larger turnouts toward the northeast gate on the south side of the road.

Within the Lamar Valley there are two campgrounds. The first is Slough Creek Campground located midway in the valley. The second is Pebble Creek Campground located further to the east toward the north-eastern gate to the park. Both are reasonably popular during the busy summer season with fishing activities. Reservations cannot be made, and these two campgrounds are both on a first-come first-serve basis. You have to be there to register for a campsite.

Drive out of the Lamar Valley the way you came in. Turn right again at that large Tower-Roosevelt intersection you saw earlier. You'll be heading west on the Upper Grand Loop Road.

Petrified Tree:

Features 🧠📷🚶

🚗 Petrified Tree entrance road will be on your left after you leave the Tower-Roosevelt junction. Turn left into this area.

①📷 The road is all of a quarter-mile long and dead ends at the Petrified Tree. Walk up the slight incline to the tree. Please respect the fence. Take pictures.

🧠 This area has been frequented by moose, especially early or late in the summer season. Watch the hill areas to the south of the Petrified Tree road for these animals. Take pictures.

🚗 When you drive out of the Petrified Tree area, turn left at the intersection with the Upper Grand Loop Road and continue to head toward Mammoth Hot Springs.

Mammoth Hot Springs:

Services

Cautions

As you enter the Mammoth Hot Springs area you'll come to an intersection. Turn left and drive towards the parking areas and park your car along the right side of the hill. RV parking at the bottom of the hill below the terraces is very limited, even for smaller RVs. The park has set aside the east side (on your left) of the road for larger vehicles, but most times cars have invaded that area too. Do the best you can when parking your RV but be ready for someone to block you in, and make it a challenge to get out of there.

Located in this part of the park is Mammoth Hot Springs, a large concentration of layered terraces of super-heated water. The water contains high concentrations of Travertine in solution which, when the water crests over the edge of each pool, drops microscopic amounts of Travertine minerals at the top edge of the pool which form the pools.

There is a National Park Service Albright Visitor Center in this part of the park. During the summer visitation season there are National Park Service rangers who can help guide you to anywhere in the park you'd like to go. Just stop in and ask.

The National Park Service Visitor Center in the Mammoth area is called the Albright Visitor Center, and its main focus is all about the history of Yellowstone National Park. Take pictures.

The Mammoth area of the park is Yellowstone National Park headquarters. You'll notice a larger presence of government vehicles in this area as well as quite an array of visitor amenities.

The terraces are best viewed from the lower area but that can change from season to season. Look for steam wafting up and that's your clue on which way to go. Walk up onto one of the boardwalks in this area, and you'll see the terraces right in front of you. Stay on the boardwalks, please. Serious damage can be done to the fragile terrace framework if you leave the boardwalks for any reason. Since the best viewing areas for the terraces change from year to year so it's always wise to ask at the National Park Service Visitor Center for the latest information. Take pictures.

Driving northward out of the main area of Mammoth Hot Springs toward the north entrance gate will take you down a short hill to the campground area. Continuing further down another hill and a curvy road, will take you past cliffs.

② 📷 This area is visited by Big Horn Sheep. You don't need binoculars here. They're easy to see, when they're there. Take pictures.

🚗 Further down the hill will take you to the north entrance station. Go ahead and exit this station and drive out to the area by the Roosevelt Arch. You can see it from the north entrance gate.

③ 📷 This is the archway that was dedicated back in 1903 by President Theodore Roosevelt as the main entrance to the park. Notice how narrow the opening is. It was built for the largest vehicles of the time – Model A Ford's – and is a bit narrow for today's modern vehicles. If you want to take pictures of the Roosevelt Arch (I can't blame you), the best thing to do is to park across the street from some of the shops in Gardiner, and walk back. The Roosevelt Arch is beautiful and historic. Take pictures.

④ 📷 If you have the time, the town of Gardiner is a quaint little town that has restaurants, gas stations, hotels, gift shops and more. This little town used to be the railroad stopping point for visitors to the park as late as the middle of the last century.

Drive back through the north entrance gate and up to the Mammoth Hot Springs area. Continue to drive south past the main part of the Mammoth area and up the hill at the south end. If you have a standard sized automobile or small truck, you can drive along the Upper Terrace Drive just south of the terraces. At the top of the hill, there's an entrance (on your right) to the Upper Terrace Loop.

DO NOT go into this drive if you're towing anything, in a bus of any sort, in an RV of any length, have a dually, or are larger than a normal vehicle. You'll see a 'restriction' sign at the entrance so if you're in a larger vehicle, park just outside the gate with all the tour buses, as the road is very narrow in spots and you WILL just get stuck – the tow bills, we've heard, are pretty stiff for a tow truck to get you out. Please don't drive in there in any vehicle larger than a normal one.

5 You can walk on the boardwalks and get into this area from the Lower Terrace boardwalk loops as well. In a normal vehicle, you can enter the gate, stay to the right and park about a hundred yards [91 meters] or so into the drive. Walk down into an older area of Mammoth Hot Springs and see what happens after eons of Travertine minerals continually depositing themselves. The area looks somewhat like the moon. Take pictures.

In the fall, during the elk rut, there are usually large concentrations of elk walking about in the Mammoth Hot Springs area. Remember I mentioned to stay a minimum of 25 yards [23 meters] away from these animals. They are capable of charging you or standing on their hind legs – much like a dog would do – and swinging their front feet at you in a bicycle type motion. The hooves on the end of those two front feet are very hard and can tear you up. If there are males present – the ones with the antlers – they are very protective of their harems of females. STAY AT LEAST 25 YARDS [23 METERS] AWAY FROM ALL ANIMALS, including the elk. Park service rangers are usually around to keep people at a safe distance. Please don't get too close as we want you to leave the park with your health intact. Thanks.

There is an amphitheater near the campground in this area of the park. There are nightly ranger-led power point presentations about historical, natural, hydrothermal, cultural, or animal related topics in the park. The programs begin at dusk and start times vary with the season, so check at one of the visitor centers for the times. You can also check for the times in the green section in the middle of the park newspaper available when you entered the park, or you can pick one up at a visitor center.

This area is one of nine locations in the park that operate the Junior Ranger Program. There is a National Park Service Visitor Center in this area where you can purchase the Junior Ranger materials for a nominal fee. A ranger can explain how the program works to your child/children. Age range is from 4 years to 13+ years of age, but it's actually fun for the whole family. So don't let age stop you from participating in the very popular Junior Ranger program. It's great!!

Located in the Mammoth Hot Springs area is the Mammoth Hot Springs Hotel. It's one of the famous old historic structures in the park. If you're looking for historic and upscale, this is the place. Located in the heart of the Mammoth area you can walk to virtually everything worth seeing in the area. This is a very popular place to stay in the park and reservations are a must during the busy season. Reservations can be made through Xanterra at 307-344-7311.

In the vicinity of the Mammoth Hot Springs area there is a campground. It's located down the first hill from the main Mammoth Hot Springs area. This is a reasonably popular campground during the summer season. Reservations cannot be made as this campground is on a first-come first-serve basis only. You have to be there to register for a campsite.

🚗 As you leave the Upper Terraces area, you'll want to go south which for most normal sized vehicles is a right turn. If you parked out by the tour buses because you are in a larger than normal vehicle, just head south away from the main Mammoth Hot Springs area.

Norris Geyser Basin Area:

🚗 As you head south on the Upper Grand Loop Road, you'll come to the Norris Geyser Basin area.

ⓘ Just north of the main intersection at Norris Geyser Basin (to your left) is the Museum of the National Park Ranger. This little building is one of the original buildings built during the time when the U.S. Army

Cavalry occupied the park and serves today as a museum to educate the public about the origins of the National Park Service and the ranger corp. There are all sorts of artifacts related to rangers in the park, information about the history of the park service, about the transition from the U.S. Army Cavalry to the National Park Service, etc. It's a pretty interesting place, if you have the time. Take pictures.

Now drive south a very short distance back on the Upper Grand Loop Road. You'll come across that same large 4-way stop intersection at Norris Geyser Basin area where you were earlier in this plan. Remember this intersection? Turn right into the basin.

There is a National Park Service Museum and Information Station in this part of the park. During the summer visitation season there are National Park Service rangers who can help guide you to anywhere in the park you'd like to go. Just stop in and ask.

This area is also very popular in the summer season and the parking lot becomes overloaded quite easily. If you see a road barrier up near the entrance to Norris Geyser Basin, this means law enforcement rangers are metering cars into and out of the parking lot to avoid gridlock. Just wait a short while out by the main intersection, and they'll let you in based on the number of cars exiting the area.

1 ♨ 🌲 Norris Geyser Basin. This is the oldest, most dramatic, and geologically active area of the park. This geyser basin is home to the world's tallest geyser – Steamboat Geyser – that erupts on a very sporadic basis. When it does go off, it's something to behold. After the initial eruptive event which lasts only a short time, the geyser goes into a steam phase with steam blasting up about 300 feet [91 meters] for about 24 hours. There's also a walkway that goes right over a geo-thermal area, as well as loads of other geysers, hot springs, and steam vents. Take pictures.

ⓘ 🚶 This area is one of nine locations in the park that operate the Junior Ranger Program. There is a National Park Service Information Station in this area where you can purchase the Junior Ranger materials for a nominal fee. A ranger can explain how the program works to your child/children. Age range is from 4 years to 13+ years of age, but it's actually fun for the whole family. So don't let age stop you from participating in the very popular Junior Ranger program. It's great!!

ⓘ 🔺 Near the Norris Geyser Basin is the Norris Campground. It's located just north of the main junction entrance to the geyser basin. This is a reasonably popular campground during the summer season.

Reservations cannot be made as this campground is on a first-come first-serve basis only. You have to be there to register for a campsite.

45 MPH / **72** KPH This is the end of this Three to Four Day Ranger Plan. I hope you had a good time, enjoyed the park, and are excited about coming back again soon. Thank you for following this plan.

Drive safely as you exit the park.

NOTE FROM THE AUTHOR

Please do me a huge favor. IF you like this book and it helped you navigate your way around Yellowstone, please, please, please ... take a moment and let the world know through social media such as Facebook, Twitter, email and text messaging, and please write a review. Thank you.

Chapter Nine

5+ Day Ranger Plan

With plenty of time to see and experience Yellowstone National Park, this plan I put together for those people who have the time to see pretty much everything: (geysers, hot springs, bubbling mud, a BIG waterfall plus several other waterfalls, a few nice hikes, terraces, and lots of wild animals).

Mark On Your Map

Old Faithful, Morning Glory Pool (hike), Grand Geyser, Kepler Cascades, Lone Star Geyser Hike, Black Sand Basin, Biscuit Basin, Mystic Falls Hike, Grand Prismatic Spring, Firehole Lake Drive, Fountain Paint Pots, Fountain Flat Drive, Firehole Canyon, Madison Junction, Gibbon Falls, Beryl Spring, Artist Paintpots, Virginia Cascades, Canyon Village Area, Hayden Valley, Mud Volcano and Sulphur Caldron Areas, Fishing Bridge Area, Lake Butte Overlook, Lake Village Area, Bridge Bay Area, Natural Bridge Hike, West Thumb Geyser Basin and Grant Village Areas, Mt. Washburn Hike, Tower Fall Area, Tower-Roosevelt Area, Lamar Valley Area, Petrified Tree, Wraith Falls and Undine Falls Hikes, Mammoth Hot Springs, Gateway Arch area, the Upper Terraces, Sheepeater Cliff, and Norris Geyser Basin and museum.

Use the map guides on the next two pages.

Mark the Ranger Day Plan stops shown here onto the park map you downloaded from the internet.

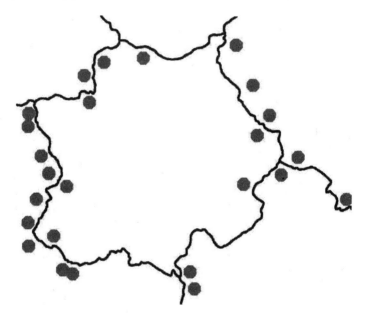

Lower Grand Loop Road

● This indicates a park feature you should highlight on a park map

Mark the Ranger Day Plan stops shown here onto the park map you downloaded from the internet.

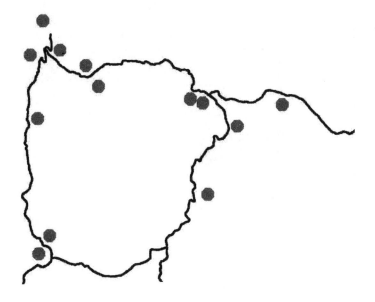

Upper Grand Loop Road

🛑 This indicates a park feature you should highlight on a park map

Old Faithful
(Upper Geyser Basin):

Look on the park map you highlighted, locate Old Faithful Geyser, and drive to this area. As you head south, or north, on Lower Grand Loop Road, you'll come across an exit that looks much like a freeway exit back home. Follow the sign for Old Faithful and exit to the east. Your adventure has begun!

There is a National Park Service Visitor Education Center in this part of the park. During the summer visitation season there are National Park Service rangers who can help guide you to anywhere in the park you'd like to go. Just stop in and ask.

The main focus of the Old Faithful Visitor Education Center focuses around the geology that

created Yellowstone National Park. From fumaroles, to steam vents, to geysers, to bubbling mud, to the volcano itself. Stop in and take a few minutes to wrap your mind around the catastrophic events that shaped the park.

1 You HAVE to take in Old Faithful Geyser. Why? Because it's Old Faithful Geyser, that's why. The geyser erupts about every 96 minutes – plus or minus 10 minutes. Each geyser eruption is dependent on the previous eruption so don't expect us to give you a "schedule." This is NOT an automated process where we push a button or use a computer for each eruption. This is totally natural and dependent on the super-heated water beneath. You can stop in at any visitor center and the rangers there will be glad to give you the next eruption time. This is one of the more important things we do. Take pictures.

2 You have enough time to walk around behind Old Faithful Geyser and look for the sign leading you up to Observation Point. You'll have to time this for about a half hour before the next eruption of the geyser. This is a short hike up onto a hill that will give you a unique view of an Old Faithful eruption. When you get up to Observation Point, sit for a while and when the eruption is near, get those cameras ready. When Old Faithful

erupts, it will erupt up to your eye level instead of erupting up and away from you, as if you were down on the viewing platform by the geyser. So you'll be even with the top of the eruption. It's a pretty neat vantage point and worth the hike up the hill. Take pictures.

You'll see that you can also continue hiking out toward Solitary Geyser. This is OK if you want to, but strongly consider having bear spray with you if you try to extend this hike on the hill any further than you have already gone. Not nearly as many people go out to Solitary Geyser as do the Observation Point hike. My take on it would be to skip the hike out to Solitary Geyser. Just think about your safety a bit, and consider what danger you may be in. It's up to you.

You have plenty of time, so after you get down to the bottom of the hill, continue walking around behind Old Faithful Geyser (stay on the trails and boardwalks). You'll see hundreds of other geo-thermal and hydro-thermal features behind Old Faithful up on Geyser Hill. Since you have the luxury of time in this Ranger Day Plan, you could actually spend an entire day just visiting the Old Faithful area. I encourage you to do exactly that if you want to. Take pictures.

Walk over to the Old Faithful Inn

– the building with a bunch of flags up on top. This is the structure that was saved from the fires of 1988 by hundreds of brave firefighters who basically put their backs to the building and any fire that was anywhere near them, they put it out. Thank you firefighters. Go into the lobby area, I'm not going to tell you where, but look for the clock. That's right ... the clock. Look around and if you can't see it, ask someone in Concierge or the gift shop where the clock is and when they show you, you'll be a bit embarrassed. It's one of those things that's right in front of your face and sometimes your eyes don't see it. Have fun with it. Take pictures.

(5) 📷 There is a short tour of the Old Faithful Inn you can take and hear all about the building, its construction, and its history. The tours are free and given by Xanterra. While you're in the lobby, if you go over to the railing area near the clock you should have found earlier, you'll notice a small sign showing the times for the building tours, or check with Concierge and ask them. While you're waiting for the tour to begin, look up, and notice that the entire roof is held up by timber and wood without many supporting posts. Yet this same roof is capable of holding immense weight when snow accumulations can be very high. It's pretty amazing. Up near the peak, you also see the walkway that

provides outside access to where the flags that run along the ridgeline of the inn are raised and lowered each day. Don't look up too long though ... you'll get a neck cramp. Take pictures.

Also, at the Old Faithful Inn, there is an outdoor viewing platform area (a parking area cover) above the drop-off area for cars and buses at the front of the building by the lobby. Go into the lobby area, walk to the back-left area of the lobby, and walk up the staircase. Walk forward and out the glass doors onto the viewing area. This is a good place to take a picnic lunch, and view Old Faithful Geyser eruptions. You can bring your own packed lunch or buy prepared meals at the cafés or delicatessens in the Inn.

 This area is one of nine locations in the park that operate the Junior Ranger Program. There is a National Park Service Visitor Center in this area where you can purchase the Junior Ranger materials for a nominal fee. A ranger can explain how the program works to your child/children. Age range is from 4 years to 13+ years of age, but it's actually fun for the whole family. So don't let age stop you from participating in the very popular Junior Ranger program. It's great!!

Old Faithful Inn is one of

approximately 900 historic buildings in the park. It was originally built back in the early 1900s and boasts beautiful, breathtaking views of Old Faithful Geyser, hundreds of geothermal and hydrothermal features, surrounding mountain areas, and is a major lodging place in this area of the park. Want to stay in a famous and historic area of the park? This is one of those places. This major hotel has it all, from upscale rooms, the finest dining, gift shops, and evening entertainment during peak season. It has a large number of rooms. Lodging here is managed by Xanterra on a reservation only basis. Xanterra can be contacted at 307-344-7311. Take pictures.

Old Faithful Lodge is available for overnight stays and features nice rooms as well as eating and dining areas. It also has a large number of rooms. Lodging here is managed by Xanterra on a reservation only basis. Xanterra can be contacted at 307-344-7311. Take pictures.

Snow Lodge is available for overnight stays and features nice rooms as well as eating and dining areas. It, too, has numerous rooms and is also open during the winter season as well. Lodging here is managed by Xanterra on a reservation only basis. Xanterra can be contacted at 307-344-7311. Take pictures.

There is no campground near the Old Faithful area.

Morning Glory Pool (hike):

Almost everyone has heard of Morning Glory Pool – some call it Morning Glory Spring – it's still the same place. It's located to the north of Old Faithful Geyser up near Daisy and Riverside geysers and it boasts bright green and yellow colors.

You can walk to it by following the trail toward Daisy and Riverside geysers. It's about a fifteen minute walk one way – if you don't get distracted by hundreds of other hydro-thermal features along the way. Morning Glory is about as bright as you can get with yellow and green bacterial mats reacting to sunlight. As with most other colorful hot springs, it needs good sunlight for the best photos. The best time of day is from about ten in the morning to about two or three in the afternoon as the sun is at its highest point. Take pictures.

Grand Geyser:

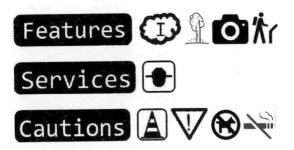

1 This geyser is located behind Old Faithful in the Upper Geyser Basin. It's a very popular geyser that erupts on a somewhat regular basis. The only problem with this geyser is that it has a 5 ½ to 7 ½ hour eruption window, and then, the accuracy is plus or minus 75 minutes. This makes it somewhat difficult for the average visitor to see the eruption, simply because it's nowhere near as "faithful" as Old Faithful. But again, you have plenty of time in this Ranger Day Plan for this experience. If you happen to be in the geyser basin and Grand Geyser is about to erupt, go for it. Get those pictures. It's called 'Grand' for a reason. It's a sizable eruption when it does come. Take pictures.

Back in your car, drive out of the Old Faithful area by exiting the parking area to your right and follow the road back to the overpass area. At the overpass area head south toward West Thumb Geyser Basin.

Kepler Cascades:

Features 🔵 〰️ 📷

Continue driving south on the Lower Grand Loop Road about two and a half to three miles [four to five kilometers]. If you look to the right, you'll see the sign for Kepler Cascades. Turn in here.

If you're interested in waterfalls, in Yellowstone National Park we have all three of the different types of waterfalls that exist in the world – right in the park. Kepler Cascades is one of those types as it's a "cascade" style waterfall. It's formed by multiple layers of volcanic lava that have eroded over time to form a waterfall that looks like water falling down a stairwell. So if you're interested in waterfalls, keep following what we'll call the "waterfall plan" and I'll take you to all three types.

1 〰️ Kepler Cascades is just south of Old Faithful Geyser in the Upper Geyser Basin on the Lower Grand Loop Road. This is a pretty waterfall that is right next to the edge of the road. Very easy to get to. Just park your car in the Kepler Cascades parking lot, walk about 50 feet [15 meters] out onto the viewing platform, and there it is. Take pictures.

If you need a restroom at this point in the day, there is a restroom about three hundred feet [91 meters] away and around the corner to the south at the trailhead area for Lone Star Geyser.

NO DRIVING TIP HERE. You can just walk over to Lone Star Geyser trailhead from the Kepler Cascades parking area. In fact, there's not much parking at the trailhead for Lone Star Geyser so it's better to just leave the car over at the Kepler Cascades parking area anyway. If you're not interested in the Lone Star Geyser hike, that's fine. Skip ahead by driving out of the Kepler Cascades parking lot and head north (to your left) on Lower Grand Loop Road.

Lone Star Geyser (hike):

Cautions Ⓐ ▽ 🚫 🚭

This is a great little hike and you have the time in this Ranger Day Plan to do this hike. The trail is almost completely flat and takes about thirty to forty minutes to get out there. The path out to the geyser is actually an old Model T Ford car road that has been changed into a biking and hiking trail. Automobiles are no longer allowed. It's about 2.4 miles [3.8 kilometers] out to the geyser so the entire hike is about 4.8 miles [7.6 kilometers]. Because the old cars didn't have much horsepower, the trail is fairly flat. And you'll be hiking through a pretty little valley with the Firehole River right next to you most of the way. This geyser is in the Old Faithful Geyser system, erupts about every 3 hours or so, and has 'major' and 'minor' eruptions.

① The first thing to do on this hike is to ask people coming back the other way on the trail if the geyser erupted and hope they say "No." This will increase your chances of seeing it erupt. The second thing to do when you arrive out at the geyser itself, is to look for a podium-like post sticking out of the ground facing the geyser. Underneath the lid of that podium is a trail log that more thoughtful hikers may have entered the last major eruption. If it last erupted at, say, 12:15 p.m. and it's now 2:55 p.m. – stick around. All you have to wait is about twenty minutes and then enjoy a fairly long eruption. Take pictures.

⬤Ⓘ 🚻 If you visited Kepler Cascades earlier, you can leave your car in that parking lot and just walk south around the end of the parking lot about a hundred feet [30 meters] to the trailhead for Lone Star Geyser. The parking lot at Lone Star Geyser is a doughnut style lot and has very little space for cars. By the way there is a restroom in the Lone Star Geyser parking area.

🚗 When you're ready to leave the Kepler Cascades parking lot, turn left and head north on the Lower Grand Loop Road.

Black Sand Basin:

🚗 Look to your left right after you pass under the Old Faithful overpass and you should see the sign for Black Sand Basin.

⊕ 🚐 NO LARGE VEHICLES are allowed in the Black Sand Basin parking area. Thanks.

① ♨ In this area there are numerous hot springs and fumaroles (steam vents). This particular basin is part of the Upper Geyser Basin where Old Faithful is located. It's called Black Sand Basin because of the sand-sized black obsidian 'sand' that appears in parts of this basin. The main hot springs in this basin are Emerald Pool (a very colorful hot spring) as well as Opalescent Pool, Cliff Geyser on the edge of Iron Creek and, of course, Handkerchief Pool. It's a very nice place to visit. Take pictures.

🚗 When you're done at Black Sand Basin, exit the parking lot and turn left to head north.

Biscuit Basin and Mystic Falls (hike):

Cautions 🅰 ⚠ 🚫 🚭

🚗 As you continue to drive north, watch on your left again for the sign to Biscuit Basin and Mystic Falls.

ℹ Biscuit Basin is also part of the Upper Geyser Basin shared by Old Faithful. Most of the thermal features in this basin tend to be smaller pools, including Silver Globe Spring, Sapphire and Black Opal Pools, as well as Jewel, Cauliflower, and Black Pearl geysers. Sapphire Pool is probably considered by most as the most interesting feature in this basin with its intensely sapphire blue water. This basin also is the location for Shell Geyser. Enjoy the area. Take pictures.

① ♨ At the back of Biscuit Basin is the trailhead for Mystic Falls. In this Ranger Day Plan you have time to hike and see this waterfall. A bit of caution here. It is OK to go on this hike if you want to but consider having bear spray with you. Not as many people go out to Mystic Falls as other places. Think about your safety a bit, and consider what danger you may be in. It's up to you. Follow the boardwalks around to the back of the basin either to the right or the left, and you'll see the trailhead. The hike is about a forty-five minute hike and does involve some uphill portions. Pace yourself and you'll see one of the nicer waterfalls in the park. Take pictures.

When you're back in your car and ready to continue, turn left out of the parking area and continue north on Lower Grand Loop Road.

Grand Prismatic Spring
(Midway Geyser Basin):

As you head north on the Lower Grand Loop Road, start looking to your left for the Grand Prismatic Spring parking area.

The parking lot here is grossly under-sized for the number of visitors to this area, so you'll have a challenge during peak usage times of the day getting a legal parking space. Please DO NOT park your car illegally as it may result in a parking citation. Thank you.

As you walk from your car, you'll cross a bridge over the Firehole River. Stand on the bridge for a few minutes. Look up and down the river. Notice that the river is smaller upstream than it is downstream. This is because Excelsior Geyser (up the rise from where the huge water flows are entering the river) is dumping approximately 4,000 gallons [15,142 liters] of super-heated water right into the Firehole River every minute. This increases the volume of the river, making it wider. It also increases the temperature of the water and there are times during the summer season when there is algae in the water north of the bridge (downstream) because of the increased temperature. Take pictures.

② ♨ At the top of the walkway just past the bridge is Excelsior Geyser. This very azure blue once active geyser now expels large volumes of water into the Firehole River. Please be mindful on windy days in this entire area to hold onto personal belongings such as hats, scarves, etc., as they can easily be blown right off you. It costs the park service lots of money to keep this geyser free of blown-in debris and it wrecks the uniqueness of this place when hats, scarves, etc are in everyone's photos. Thank you. Take pictures.

③ ♨ Continue up the boardwalk where you'll come to the multi-colored Grand Prismatic Spring. This is a major attraction in the park. Again, hold onto your hats, scarves, etc. On warmer, less windy days, the steam is reduced and it's easier to see the spring itself. The opposite is true on cooler days. The steam will fog up your camera lens and eyeglasses in a heartbeat, making it a challenge to take good pictures. As with most other colorful hot springs, it needs good sunlight for the best photos so between about ten in the morning and mid-afternoon sometime are the best photo opportunities. STAY ON THE BOARDWALK AND DON'T TOUCH THE WATER!! Take pictures.

It's common for people to want to take a photo of Grand Prismatic Spring from an elevated area. These types of photos are in many publications. The problem with this is the hillside has been unstable for years. There has been significant damage to resources and visitor safety concerns have also been an issue for quite some time. Park administration worked diligently to come up with a solution to this dilemma. In a collaborative effort between geologists, park administration, trail crews from Montana Conservation Corps and Yellowstone Youth Conservation Corps, a new trail has been completed to an overlook with a view of Grand Prismatic Spring and the Midway Geyser Basin. The new trail is 105 feet [32 meters] high and just over one half mile long from the

Fairy Falls Trail. The Fairy Falls parking area has also been redone to allow parking near the trailhead. So it's now possible to take great pictures of the spring and be safe at the same time. Please stay on this new trail to avoid further resource damage and possible fines. Thank you.

As you leave the parking lot at Grand Prismatic Spring, turn left and go north on the Lower Grand Loop Road.

Firehole Lake Drive:

As you drive north from the Grand Prismatic Spring area, you'll see the sign for Firehole Lake Drive. Turn right IF you have a normal-sized vehicle. Sorry ... NO large vehicles.

1 After making the right turn onto Firehole Lake Drive (in your regular sized vehicle), continue on. This drive includes

going past more hydro-thermal and geo-thermal features including Great Fountain Geyser, White Dome Geyser, and Firehole Lake at the back end of this loop. Great Fountain Geyser doesn't erupt very often, but when it does ... it's spectacular. Eruption times are available at any of the visitor centers in the park. Take pictures.

At the end of this one-way drive you'll find yourself just across from Fountain Paint Pots. You'll also see you can't cut across the intersection legally to enter that area. SO, turn left at this intersection and go south for a couple hundred yards [183 meters], or so, and turn right into the far end of the parking area for Fountain Paint Pots. See how easy that was?

Fountain Paint Pots
(Lower Geyser Basin):

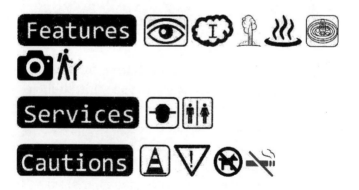

As you drive north, you'll see a sign for Fountain Paint Pots and Lower Geyser Basin. Turn left into the SOUTH end of this parking lot. Remember this entrance area as this is where you'll exit later.

The parking lot here is grossly under-sized for the number of visitors to this area, so you'll have a challenge during peak usage times of the day getting a legal parking space. Please **DO NOT** park your car illegally as it may result in a parking citation. Thank you.

1 As you walk up the boardwalk you'll come to Silex Spring on your right. Take pictures.

2 The next thing you'll see, up and to your left, is bubbling mud at Fountain Paint Pots. If you watch very carefully and stare at the middle of the bubbling pots, you'll see one or more pots actually spit up a small ball of molten mud about the size of a quarter. It happens about every minute or two. Don't get discouraged if nothing happens, because sometimes conditions are just not right. Take pictures.

3 Walk around and take in all the hot springs, steam vents (fumaroles), and small geysers in this area. Some are below and near the lower portion of the boardwalk when standing near Fountain Paint Pots. Walk down there. Take pictures.

4 Following the upper boardwalk near the Fountain Paint Pot feature, walk out the boardwalk to the west and down the stairs to Clepsydra Geyser. You'll witness a fairly regular eruption of hot steam and water that ejects out the top of this geyser. Take pictures.

When you're done visiting the Fountain Paint Pot area, drive to the SOUTH end of the parking area and exit the parking area by turning left (you can't turn left at the north end of the parking area). Continue heading north on the Lower Grand Loop Road.

Fountain Flat Drive:

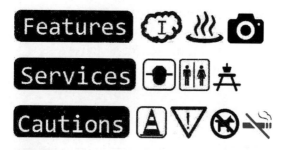

Fountain Flat Drive will be on your left after the large open meadow just north of Fountain Paint

Pots. Turn left into the area.

Near the entrance of Fountain Flat Drive is a picnic area. During the heavy usage periods in the summer this is fairly congested. Because of the proximity to the river, families enjoy this area. So enjoy a nice picnic lunch with the kids playing in the river. Remember, no floaties! Take pictures (and don't forget to dry the kids off)!

1 About halfway along this drive is the site of the former Fountain Flats Hotel (no longer there). It would have been to your right about the time the road starts curving to the left just after you pass the entrance to the picnic area.

2 About a quarter of a mile into the drive, at the end, there is an under-used parking area. This is a great place to park your car for hikes to Ojo Caliente Spring (on your right just before the foot bridge), Fairy Falls, Queens Laundry (via the Sentinel Meadows trail), and the Sentinel Meadows area. You have time in this Ranger Day Plan to spend some time hiking in this area. The Fairy Falls portion of this trail is also set aside as a bicycle trail, if you are inclined. Take pictures.

If you do decide to hike a bit in this area, there is a lake along the main trail (on your left) called Goose Lake which has been a site for a nesting pair of Bald

Eagles, but the nest isn't always consistently occupied. Take pictures.

When exiting this area with your car, turn left at the junction with Lower Grand Loop Road.

Firehole Canyon Drive:

Continue to drive north on Lower Grand Loop Road and you'll come upon a sign on your left for Firehole Canyon Drive. If you're in a normal size vehicle, turn left and drive in.

NO LARGE VEHICLES on Firehole Canyon Drive!! Law enforcement watches this area fairly closely. As with some other areas of the park, getting stuck in a large vehicle prohibited area can be a pretty hefty tow bill. So please don't go in if you're in a large vehicle. Thanks.

About a quarter of a mile into this drive, you'll see the Firehole River on your right. The road will dip down to just about the height of the river. Look around, as you're inside the volcano, and it looks like it. Take pictures.

2 About halfway into the drive, you'll come to Firehole Falls on your right with the parking area on the left. This is one of the more impressive waterfalls in the park. Please don't hike down the hill towards the river as this is a closed area. Take your pictures from the roadway.

3 Near the end of this drive, you'll come up to a swimming hole set aside by the park for visitors. Enjoy yourself and cool off. BUT, be aware that this feature is not open all summer long. It's closed whenever high water or swift current become a safety issue – so check with a visitor center before getting into the water and take notice of any signage posted at the top of the stairway or elsewhere in that area. If the entrance to the stairway is blocked off – the area is CLOSED.

Also, park your car LEGALLY in this area and please don't encroach on the roadway. Keep those tires outside the white line or you can be cited for impeding traffic flow. Thank you. IF you decide to swim be aware there is no lifeguard on duty and swimming is at your own risk. Diving from the rocks is prohibited and one of the things rangers are watching for. Be aware that any type of flotation device is also prohibited as they sometimes get away from visitors and when they float downstream they end up tangled in the pumps of a local fish hatchery. It's expensive to repair those pumps, so please ... NO FLOATIES!!

At the end of the one-way road through Firehole Canyon, turn left at the stop sign and continue north on the Lower Grand Loop Road.

Madison Junction:

Right after you drive down a small hill and cross a bridge over the Gibbon River, you'll climb the small hill on the opposite side. Near the top of that hill is the turnoff for Madison Junction. Turn left.

Madison Junction is named for the

confluence of the Firehole and Gibbon Rivers that join to become the Madison River. This is a world class fly fishing area. The Firehole River comes from the southern portion of the park – where a large concentration of geysers and hydro-thermal features are – and it winds its way northward to the Madison Junction. The Gibbon River comes from the central portion of the park before it arrives at the Madison Junction. When the two rivers meet, they become the Madison River, also known as the Madison Junction. It's the meeting of the two rivers that is the "junction," NOT the road junction. The Madison Junction area is also home to the "campfire myth" said to have taken place here. Ask any ranger and they should be able to share with you the background of the "campfire myth." As a ranger, take it from me, it's pretty interesting. Take pictures.

There is a National Park Service Information Station in this part of the park. During the summer visitation season there are National Park Service rangers who can help guide you to anywhere in the park you'd like to go. Just stop in and ask.

(1) While you're at the Madison Junction area, look westward down the canyon toward the town of West Yellowstone. Notice on your left (south) the mountain vegetation – mostly Lodgepole Pine trees – is generally non-existent, yet on the right (north) the trees flourish. You're standing at one of several areas in the park where you can see

the aftermath of the fires of 1988 that destroyed about one third of the park. The park is just about 2.2 million acres, and the fires of 1988 consumed about 800,000 acres. Looking to your left again, further down the mountain and even with the bottom of the valley floor, you'll notice fairly large Lodgepole Pine trees here, yet this was a burn area. How can that be? Well, the trees down low are the babies of the burned trees and are being fed a constant diet of nutrients from the Gibbon and Firehole Rivers, but the trees up on the slope of the edge of the volcano – again on the left side of the valley – are barely surviving and are much less tall because of lack of nutrients. This demonstrates the stark difference between having good nutrients in the soil and not – all because of the fire of 1988. Fires in the park actually help the ecosystem.

There is an amphitheater near the campground and the Information Station in this area of the park. There are nightly ranger-led power point presentations about historical, natural, hydrothermal, cultural, or animal related topics in the park. The programs begin at dusk and start times vary with the season, so check at one of the visitor centers for the times. You can also check for the times in the green section in the middle of the park newspaper available when you entered the park, or you can pick one up at a visitor center.

This area is one of nine locations in the park that operate the Junior Ranger Program. There is a National Park Service Information Station in this area where you can purchase the Junior Ranger materials for a nominal fee. A ranger can explain how the program works to your child/children. Age range is from 4 years to 13+ years of age, but it's actually fun for the whole family. So don't let age stop you from participating in the very popular Junior Ranger program. It's great!!

In the Madison Junction area of the park there is Madison Campground. This particular campground has some spaces large enough for smaller RVs but is mostly sized for tent and tent trailer camping. The campground is just adjacent to the Madison Junction parking lot and is located just west of the intersection heading toward the town of West Yellowstone. Reservations can be made through Xanterra at 307-344-7311.

When done at the Madison Junction area, get in your car and turn left when leaving the parking lot. You'll go past the road junction that heads back to the town of West Yellowstone (don't turn here) and continue north on the Lower Grand Loop Road.

Gibbon Falls:

Features ⟨I⟩ 🌊 📷

Services ⊟

Cautions ⚠

🚗 About six miles [9.5 kilometers] north of Madison Junction, you'll come to Gibbon Falls on the east side of the road. Turn right into the parking area.

①🌊 This is a pretty waterfall and a nice place to stretch your legs. It is also one of those areas that if you have an animal that needs to be walked, you can do so if you're never any further than 100 feet [30 meters] from a developed area. Be mindful of the distance though. Some people do go all the way down to the far end of the walkway to get a great picture, but are well past the 100 feet [30 meters] maximum distance from the parking lot. Please pick up after your animal. It's also an area rangers like to rove around quite a bit more than some other areas and answer visitors' questions about the park. From this area, looking to the south along the ridges of the mountains, you can also see the remnants of the last volcanic eruption

640,000 years ago. Take pictures.

 If you need a restroom in this area of the park, there is no restroom right at Gibbon Falls. But just to the north up the road about a quarter mile on your left is Iron Spring picnic area, and there is a restroom there.

From the Gibbon Falls area, turn right out of the parking lot back onto the Lower Grand Loop Road and head north again.

Beryl Spring:

Beryl Spring is right along the roadway on the left side of the road, a few miles north of Gibbon Falls. You'll probably see the steam before you see the bridge or the spring. Pull off to the left side of the roadway and park your car.

The spring is just adjacent to the Gibbon

River. The spring drains into the river and produces quite a bit of steam, even on moderately warm summer days. There is a short bridge right next to the spring, which can make the drive over the bridge with a vehicle a challenge because of the 'London fog' amounts of steam wafting right over the roadway on the bridge. The spring is on your left.

(1) ♨ This is a short stop. Walk a couple of hundred feet [61 meters] up near the bridge, and enjoy one of Yellowstone's lesser viewed springs but a nice one just the same. Take pictures.

🚗 When you're done at Beryl Spring, continue driving north on the Lower Grand Loop Road.

Artist Paintpots:

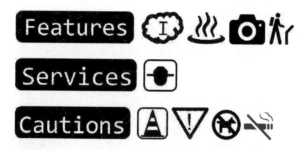

🚗 Just north of Gibbon Falls you'll come across Artist Paintpots. The paintpots are on the right side of the road. Turn right into the parking area. Sometimes this little parking area overflows and parking is a challenge. Try to park legally.

(I) Years ago this area was very active with multi-colored pools of very hot water bubbling and churning all over the place. Today it has quieted down a bit and is still a nice place to visit, but it's nowhere near what it used to be.

(1) The short hike out to the paintpots is about a quarter of a mile in length and fairly flat. A pretty easy trail. No dogs or smoking are allowed on this trail as with most features and trails in the park.

(2) Out at the viewing area there is a short loop trail up onto a small hill above and behind the paintpots that provides a nice place for photos looking down into the paintpot area. Take pictures.

From the Artist Paint Pots area, continue to drive north to the Norris Geyser Basin intersection. Turn right at this large 4-way stop intersection and head east towards Canyon Village. Don't worry about Norris Geyser Basin right now as we'll come back to this area later on.

Virginia Cascades:

About five or six miles [9.5 kilometers] down the road from the Norris Geyser Basin intersection, you'll see a sign for Virginia Cascades Drive. With your normal sized vehicle, bear to the right (it's a slight "Y" intersection) onto the two mile, or so, one-way cascades drive.

This one-way road is a great little side jaunt but NO LARGE VEHICLES! If you're in a large vehicle just keep heading east toward Canyon Village. Please don't go in Virginia Cascades.

This short little road takes you past one of the "cascade" style waterfalls in the park formed by multiple layers of lava flows thousands of years ago that created small shelves of volcanic rock that the Gibbon River runs over. It's like water running down a stairwell. This creates the effect referred to as a cascade. Take pictures.

🚗 When you're done at Virginia Cascades and at the end of the one-way drive, turn right to get back onto the Grand Loop Road and head east towards Canyon Village.

Canyon Village Area:

🚗 As you're coming into the Canyon Village area, turn right at the large 4-way stop intersection and drive south toward Fishing Bridge on the Lower Grand Loop Road.

🏛 There is a National Park Service Visitor Education Center in this part of the park. During the summer visitation season there are National Park Service rangers who can help guide you to anywhere in the park you'd like to go. Just stop in and ask.

💭 The Canyon Village Visitor Education

Center's main focus is all about the volcano. From the first eruption about 2.1 million years ago to the last eruption 640,000 years ago, this educational experience takes you all the way through. This is powerful. Take pictures.

Located in the Canyon Village area is the largest waterfall in the 'front country' area of the park. It's called Lower Falls and can be viewed best from Artist Point. The waterfall is 308 feet high, or 94 meters, and at its peak the average flow of the Yellowstone River is around 63,500 gallons per second, or for you metrically challenged folks, that's more than 240,000 liters per second. At some parts of the season the flow is much higher IF there has been an unusually high snowfall the previous winter.

The third left turn is called South Rim Drive with a sign saying "Artist Point." The parking lot for Artist Point – all the way at the end of this drive – is pretty good sized for automobiles and small RVs. Be careful if you're in a larger RV as there is limited parking for larger vehicles like RVs and tour buses. This lot also fills to capacity during the busy summer months.

After parking in the main lot, walk to the east a couple of hundred yards [183 meters] over to the Lower Falls viewing platform which has a lower and upper viewing area to take pictures. This area IS handicap accessible. Take pictures.

⚠️ Don't stand on the stone walls as it's unsafe, a LONG way down, and probably not survivable.

🄸 📷 While at Artist Point you have a wonderful and dramatic view of Grand Canyon of the Yellowstone. At the viewing area between the waterfall and where you're standing is the start of the "grand canyon." If you walk around to the back side of the viewing area, you can see more of the canyon as it continues downstream. Take pictures.

🚗 On your way back from Artist Point, you could stop at Uncle Tom's Trail and take the trail down to a great view of Lower Falls. There's also a nice view of Upper Falls without taking Uncle Tom's Trail.

②🌊🚶 This hike is pretty challenging and includes trails, metal walkways, and an expanded metal staircase attached to the side of a huge boulder with loads of steps. It's about 500 feet [152 meters] down and about 328 steps. If you're uneasy about this, ask others coming back up what it was like, and make a decision from there. The view, though, is worth it because down on the viewing platform you'll find yourself about halfway down the full height of Lower Falls looking right at the falls itself. Now be aware there are times of the year this walkway is closed as the mist coming off the falls is too much for safe passage. The metal stairways can become slick and can also freeze. Take pictures.

3 While you're in the same Uncle Tom's Trail parking lot, stroll over to the viewpoint for Upper Falls – it's about a hundred feet [30 meters], or so, off to the left. Upper Falls and Lower Falls are both along the Yellowstone River. So the same 63,500 gallons [240,000 liters] of water per second flows over both waterfalls. The view is amazing. Upper Falls is 109 feet high, or about 33 meters. Take pictures.

Turn right out of the Uncle Tom's Trail parking lot and return back to the main Lower Grand Loop Road. Turn right and drive to the next right turn. This is Brink of the Upper Falls.

4 There is a short hike down to the top of the falls that has a pretty nice view. The hike is about 60 feet [18 meters] down and about a hundred yards [91 meters] long. When you get to the brink area look upstream. You'll notice a particularly unusual site. As the river comes down through the canyon it zig-zags back and forth, and each time it turns there is a bluff hiding the turn of the water. This is because eons of water erosion changed the course of the river. The erosion and the 'turn' of the river hidden behind the bluff creates the unusual effect of making it appear that the river is colliding with itself as it zig-zags its way down the canyon before making the final turn right in front of you, then over the brink. Take pictures.

Drive back to the main loop road again and turn right yet again. This will take you north again toward Canyon Village area. Turn right where the sign says "North Rim Drive" and "Brink of the Lower Falls." You'll see a parking lot right away, and this is where you should try and park. This parking lot fills to capacity quite often so do the best you can.

Lower Falls is the tallest waterfall in Yellowstone Park in the front country at 308 feet [94 meters] high and, again, about 63,500 gallons [240,000 liters] of water per second go over the top.

The walkway is near the start of this parking lot on the south side. The hike down to Brink of the Lower Falls can be challenging. It's about 250 to 300 feet [76 to 91 meters] down and the trail is a switchback style trail. But remember, you're at almost 8,000 feet [2,413 meters] elevation. Stand at the top of the trail and decide if you can make the journey. It's well worth it IF you can do it. Ask others that are coming back up how hard it was for them and make your decision from there. If you decide to go down, you'll be standing at the very top of the waterfall with all that water rushing right past you before it falls over the brink. It's pretty impressive. Take pictures.

Back in your car, continue to drive along North Rim Drive as it's a one-way road anyway. There are "Lookout Point" and "Grand View" viewing areas with good photo opportunities of Grand Canyon of the Yellowstone along the way. Why not stop as you can always delete the picture(s) later if you don't want them, right? As you continue along North Rim Drive you'll also see the sign on your right for "Inspiration Point," so make the right turn and drive out to the parking lot at the end.

6 Inspiration Point is another fantastic view up and down Grand Canyon of the Yellowstone. The Minnetaree Indians called the area "Mi tse a-da-zi," which means "Rock Yellow River." Yellowstone's version of the Grand Canyon in Arizona, is called Grand Canyon of the Yellowstone and is about 22 miles [35 kilometers] long and follows the Yellowstone River up to Tower Fall area, which we'll talk about later on. Take pictures.

Drive your car back to the intersection with the one-way road and turn right. As you continue to follow North Rim Drive, the one-way road will take you back to the Canyon Village area where the National Park Service Visitor Center is located as well as food, restrooms, gift shops, a post office, and the lodges. Most of these areas will be on your left as you enter the area. This area IS handicap accessible. The gas station, campground, and amphitheater will be on your right.

You may be wondering why I have you back-tracking. This is because if you get to Lower Falls too late in the day, the picture quality will go way down as the sun would be getting too close to the horizon and foul up your photos. Please forgive me.

If you've been following along the plan so far, you've now seen two "cascade" style waterfalls at Kepler Cascades and Virginia Cascades, and two "regular" waterfalls at Lower and Upper Falls. Keep going, you're doing great!

There is an amphitheater near the campground in this area of the park. There are nightly ranger-led power point presentations about historical, natural, hydrothermal, cultural, or animal related topics in the park. The programs begin at dusk and start times vary with the season, so check at one of the visitor centers for the times. You can also check for the times in the green section in the middle of the park newspaper available when you entered the park, or you can pick one up at a visitor center.

This area has one of nine locations in the park that operate the Junior Ranger Program. There is a National Park Service Visitor Center in Canyon Village where you can purchase the Junior Ranger materials for a nominal fee. A ranger can explain how the program works to your child/children. Age range is from 4 years to 13+ years of age, but it's actually fun for the whole family. So don't let age stop you from participating in the very popular Junior Ranger program. It's great!!

The Canyon Village area has plenty of lodging available at Canyon Lodge but during the summer season everything is booked solid so if you want to stay in this part of the park you'll have to book early. Canyon Lodge just completed a major addition of hundreds of rooms that are brand new. This is a very popular place to stay in the park and reservations are a must during the busy season. Reservations can be made through Xanterra at 307-344-7311.

Canyon Village also has a nice campground complex. The campground here is located north of the main intersection near the gas station. Like Madison Campground, it too can handle some smaller RVs but is designed mostly for tent and tent trailer camping. Reservations can be made through Xanterra at 307-344-7311.

🚗 When you're done in the Canyon Village area, drive back out to that large 4-way stop intersection and turn left. You'll be heading south on the Lower Grand Loop Road.

Hayden Valley:

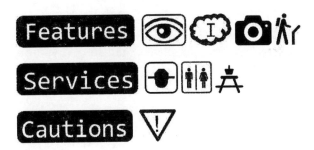

🚗 Continue heading south from the Canyon Village area on the Lower Grand Loop Road. After going about three or four miles [six kilometers], you'll be entering the Hayden Valley area.

ⓘ Hayden Valley is named for Ferdinand Vandeveer Hayden who in 1871 led one of first surveys of Yellowstone National Park and the surrounding area. Hayden was a geologist and was federally funded to document the area for possible legislation to create the park.

① ⚠ 📷 Hayden Valley has lots of WILD animals. The primary animals that roam this area are bison, elk, wolves and an occasional grizzly bear. Seasonally, there are sometimes black bear and moose in the area as well. You'll probably get into animal jams (traffic jams caused by animals) as visitors take photos of wild animals. Watch the car in front of you! Most times the animals are a ways away and easy to photograph. Sometimes they're right up on the roadway and people get WAY TOO CLOSE to them for their own safety. People DO get injured when attacked. Please stay a MINIMUM of 100 yards [91 meters] from bears and wolves and 25 yards [23 meters] away from ALL OTHER wild animals. Drive safely, keep your distance from animals, and take pictures.

🚗 You've been driving south on the Lower Grand Loop Road. Just keep driving south heading towards the Mud Volcano area.

Mud Volcano and Sulphur Caldron:

Cautions 🅰️ ⚠️ 🚫 🚭

🚗 Park your car in the main Mud Volcano parking area. It will be just past the Sulphur Caldron area (on your left), but DON'T PARK in the Sulphur Caldron parking area. Just continue down the road about a hundred yards [91 meters] and the main lot will be off to your right. It's a pretty good sized lot so you shouldn't have too much trouble.

ℹ️ In this area there are two wonderful thermal features – Mud Volcano and Sulphur Caldron. The Mud Volcano area has a nice sized parking lot and it's usually pretty easy to find parking in this area.

① ♨️ 🌀 Walk up onto the small mountain or large hill – whichever way you want to look at it – and enjoy bubbling mud pots, small caldrons, Dragon's Breath, fumaroles (steam vents), and a whole array of other geo-thermal and hydro-thermal features. You'll also enjoy the aromatic odor of sulphur, thanks to Mother Nature. The aromatic aroma in this area is probably the strongest in the park. Enjoy!

② 🌀 When you come down the Mud Volcano hill on the boardwalk, you'll notice a small parking lot on the opposite side of the road and just a bit to the north that looks like overflow parking for the main lot. Don't be fooled! It is NOT overflow parking and many people make the mistake of thinking it is – so they take off and miss a wonderful feature of the park. Just leave your car in the main Mud Volcano parking lot and walk across the Lower Grand Loop Road – WATCH OUT FOR TRAFFIC – as people zip right through this area. After you're across the road, walk up a slight hill to your left and over to the stone wall and look down. You'll see two huge bubbling mud caldrons. This is Sulphur Caldron. Take pictures as this is a feature you'll be glad you didn't miss.

Please DO NOT take your RV (small or not) over to the parking area near Sulphur Caldron. There is limited parking there at best and an RV in this area will probably get blocked in by other vehicles. Please just walk over to Sulphur Caldron from the main parking lot at Mud Volcano. Thanks.

After you get back into your car, turn right out of the Mud Volcano parking lot and head south on the Lower Grand Loop Road toward Fishing Bridge.

Fishing Bridge Area:

Watch for the sign for the Fishing Bridge area. The turn into the Fishing Bridge area is a left turn.

There is a National Park Service Museum and Visitor Center in this part of the park. During the summer visitation season there are National Park Service rangers who can help guide you to anywhere in the park you'd like to go. Just stop in and ask.

The Fishing Bridge Museum and Visitor Center's main focus is on fishing and the history in this area of the park. It's very interesting and informative. Fishing Bridge itself is an old historic bridge that in the not-too-distant past allowed fishing right from the bridge (hence the name). There are native Cutthroat Trout swimming in and out of the lake and into the Yellowstone River constantly. It WAS a great place to fish – BUT – too many issues with traffic congestion, tangled fishing lines, and upset visitors have changed all of that. Fishing Bridge is now CLOSED to fishing of any kind. Please obey the signs. Thanks. Take pictures.

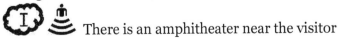 There is an amphitheater near the visitor

center in this area of the park. There are nightly ranger-led power point presentations about historical, natural, hydrothermal, cultural, or animal related topics in the park. The programs begin at dusk and start times vary with the season, so check at one of the visitor centers for the times. You can also check for the times in the green section in the middle of the park newspaper available when you entered the park, or you can pick one up at a visitor center.

This area has one of nine locations in the park that operate the Junior Ranger Program. There is a National Park Service Visitor Center in Fishing Bridge where you can purchase the Junior Ranger materials for a nominal fee. A ranger can explain how the program works to your child/children. Age range is from 4 years to 13+ years of age, but it's actually fun for the whole family. So don't let age stop you from participating in the very popular Junior Ranger program. It's great!!

There are showers and laundry facilities in this area of the park.

If you need postal service or medical clinic facilities you'll have to make the short drive over to the Lake Village area for these services.

The Fishing Bridge Campground is the only one like it in the entire park. This campground is set up for hard-sided recreational vehicles ONLY. There are no tent spaces in this campground. It's also very popular during the busy summer season. Reservations can be made through Xanterra at 307-344-7311.

(1) 🚶 📷 Just east of the main Fishing Bridge area is a short kid-friendly hike out to Storm Point. Look for the small parking area for Indian Pond (on your right when going to the east). When you walk out to the point, if it's a nice warm day, keep an eye out for Marmots – there are hundreds of them. The warm summer days bring them out for some much needed vitamin D (just kidding – they probably just want to warm up a bit). The kids usually get a kick out of seeing them. Please don't feed them though as we don't want them to become aggressive looking for 'human food' from visitors who come there in the future. Thanks.

📷 Also out at the end of the Storm Point trail is a great opportunity for a very nice picture of Yellowstone Lake. The sun rises and sets away from the direction you're taking your shot – you'd be pointing your camera/cell phone toward the south – so you won't get any reflection from the sun in your photo. If it's a clear day the Grand Teton Mountains will be in the background. Take pictures.

(2) 🚶 Also as you wind your way back

around to the west, you'll follow the trail into a wooded area. This is a nice, quiet, peaceful little walk of about a quarter-mile which opens up at the end to a small meadow and the trail then comes back on itself to the main trail you walked out on originally. Take pictures.

From the Storm Point area if you're in a normal size vehicle head east toward the east entry gate and Cody, Wyoming. If you're in a LARGE VEHICLE, please just head back towards the Fishing Bridge area and turn left after crossing Fishing Bridge itself.

Lake Butte Overlook:

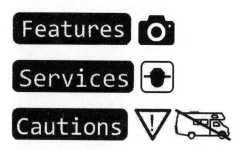

As you drive east in a normal vehicle on the east entrance road towards Cody, Wyoming, you'll see the sign for Lake Butte Overlook. Turn left and drive up the hill. NO LARGE VEHICLES are allowed as the grade is too great. If you're in a large vehicle, please don't try this hill. Thanks.

①📷 This is a great place for scenic views of the park. At the top of Lake Butte Overlook looking to the south – on a clear day – you'll have Yellowstone Lake in the foreground, the park's Red Mountain range in the mid-ground, and the Grand Tetons in the background of any photos you take. It's a real nice place to have a picnic lunch and enjoy the views. Dress in layers though, as it gets pretty breezy up there, and sometimes the temperature is much cooler than down below. Take pictures.

🚗 At the bottom of the hill at Lake Butte Overlook, you'll need to turn to the right and head back toward the Fishing Bridge area. When you arrive at the intersection with the Lower Grand Loop Road just west of Fishing Bridge itself, turn left and head south again.

Lake Village Area:

Cautions ⚠️

🚗 As you drive south on the Lower Grand Loop Road, the sign for Lake Village is about three miles [4.8 kilometers] south of the turn you just made. Turn left into the Lake Village area.

① 🛏️ The Lake Hotel is one of the famous historic buildings in the park. It was originally built back in the early 1900s and is the site of motion pictures, beautiful breathtaking views of the lake and surrounding mountains, and is a major lodging area in the park. Want to stay in a historic area of the park? This is one of those places. This major hotel has it all, from upscale rooms, the finest dining, gift shops, and evening entertainment during peak season. It has a large number of rooms available during the summer season, and is NOT open during the winter season. Lodging here is managed by Xanterra on a reservation only basis. Xanterra can be contacted at 307-344-7311. Take pictures.

② 🛏️ Lake Lodge is also one of the famous historic buildings in the park. It, too, has beautiful breathtaking views of the lake and surrounding mountains, and is a major lodging area in this part of the park. This is also one of those 'must see' places. Lodging here is also managed by Xanterra on a reservation only basis. Xanterra can be contacted at 307-344-7311. Take pictures.

Lake Hotel and Lake Lodge both have dining rooms and are very nice places to dine. Both structures are historic. Upscale menus, great views, and ambiance await you. Reservations are managed by Xanterra and can be made via phone at 307-344-7311. Take pictures.

There are also cabins for rent during the peak summer season in this area of the park. Reservations are managed by Xanterra and can be made via phone at 307-344-7311.

If you need fuel, there is a gas station in the area but you'll have to make the short drive over to the Fishing Bridge area for this service.

As you leave the Lake Village area, turn left again and head south on the Lower Grand Loop Road.

Bridge Bay Area:

Services

Cautions

The Bridge Bay area will be on your right and just a short distance from the Lake Village area. Turn right into the area when you see the sign.

This is the only place in the park where a marina is associated with Yellowstone Lake. This is a good sized marina where you can moor and launch your own boat, rent boats and watercraft, and is a major hub for fishing activities in the lake. This is also where you can take a guided tour of the lake (all these activities are for a fee). Reservations can be made through Xanterra at 307-344-7311. Take pictures.

There is an amphitheater near the campground in this area of the park. There are nightly ranger-led power point presentations about historical, natural, hydrothermal, cultural, or animal related topics in the park. The programs begin at dusk and start times vary with the season, so check at one of the visitor centers for the times. You can also check for the times in the green section in the middle of the park newspaper available when you entered the park, or you can pick one up at a visitor center.

⊂I⊃ 🛏 Lodging (other than the campground) is over in the Lake Village area just adjacent to the Bridge Bay area. You'll have to make the short drive over there.

⊂I⊃ ▲ The Bridge Bay Campground can handle a few smaller RVs but is mostly designed for tent camping or tent trailers. It's also very popular during the busy summer season. Reservations can be made through Xanterra at 307-344-7311.

⊂I⊃ ⛽ If you need fuel there is a gas station in the area but you'll have to make the short drive over to the Fishing Bridge area for this service.

🚗 IF you decide you want to skip the Natural Bridge hike, drive out of the Bridge Bay area and turn right and head south on the Lower Grand Loop Road.

Natural Bridge (hike):

237

① Of all the day hikes in the park, this is one of the better ones. It's right in the Bridge Bay area. Natural Bridge is a hole in a small mountain in this part of the park. The hike is about two and a half miles [about four kilometers] each way and takes about two hours or so depending on how much time you spend looking at the hole. Finding the trailhead is another story, though, so listen up. If you're already in the Bridge Bay area, drive past the entrance to the campground and park your car in the Bridge Bay Marina parking lot. You should see the top half of the marina building from your car. If you're looking at the marina building, the trailhead is behind you at the back of the parking lot. Hop onto the trail and enjoy the hike.

① 🚶 As you follow the trail, you'll be walking through lots of trees and shade, and there may also be other hikers in this area. It's not a hugely popular hike, but it's still a nice one. When you get out to the base of the small mountain, look up and you'll see the Natural Bridge (the hole) in the mountain. From that vantage point the hole is a bit of a challenge to see, but you can see it. For a better view, hike to your right as there is a loop trail that takes you up and onto the top of the mountain. Now you can see down through the hole at the base area you left earlier. Good views up there. Stay safe and take pictures.

⚠️ We've been asked about bear spray on this hike and this is one hike you should think about it. We've never really had a problem in that area and I've been on this trail lots of times and have never seen a bear. But there's always a first time for everything. It's your decision.

🚗 IF you opted to do the Natural Bridge hike, drive out of the Bridge Bay area and turn right and head south on the Lower Grand Loop Road.

West Thumb Geyser Basin and Grant Village:

🚗 As you drive south on the Lower Grand Loop Road, watch for the signs directing you into the West Thumb Geyser Basin and Grant Village areas.

There is a National Park Service Visitor Center in this part of the park at Grant Village. There is also a National Park Service Information Station in the West Thumb Geyser Basin. During the summer visitation season there are National Park Service rangers who can help guide you to anywhere in the park you'd like to go. Just stop in and ask.

West Thumb Geyser Basin. This is home to the most recent volcanic activity in the park, which was a huge lava flow about 70,000 years ago preceded by earlier lava flows about 174,000 years ago. The geyser basin has several hot springs and steam vents along with other great features to look at. Take pictures.

Fishing Cone Geyser is located in West Thumb Geyser Basin near the bottom edge of the boardwalk just off the shore into Yellowstone Lake. There is a photo taken about a hundred years ago and a short story of a guy standing on top of the geyser – you are NOT allowed to do this today – and he's fishing. So, as the story goes he catches a fish, dunks it in the geyser – which does what? That's right ... dunking the fish into the geyser cooks the fish. He then tosses out another baited line, and while he's waiting to catch the next fish, he can eat the one he just caught. Check out the picture and story in front of this feature. Take pictures.

② **📷** Drive along Yellowstone Lake for beautiful views of this stunning alpine lake. This lake is the largest lake in North America above 7,000 feet (2,133 meters) elevation, making it an alpine lake. Feel free to stop at one of the many turnouts in this area (please keep all four wheels of your vehicle outside the white line at the edge of the roadway or you could be subject to a citation for impeding traffic flow), take your shoes off, and enjoy a rather brisk dip in the lake. Warning: depending upon the time of year, this is a very cold lake and getting in further than your knees is not recommended as hypothermia can easily set in. Take pictures.

There is an amphitheater near the campground and the Grant Village Visitor Center in this area. There are nightly ranger-led power point presentations about historical, natural, hydrothermal, cultural, or animal related topics in the park. The programs begin at dusk and start times vary with the season, so check at one of the visitor centers for the times. You can also check green section in the middle of the park newspaper available when you entered the park, or you can pick one up at a visitor center.

This area has two of nine locations in the park that operate the Junior

Ranger Program. There is a National Park Service Visitor Center in Grant Village and an Information Station in West Thumb where you can purchase the Junior Ranger materials for a nominal fee. A ranger can explain how the program works to your child/children. Age range is from 4 years to 13+ years of age, but it's actually fun for the whole family. So don't let age stop you from participating in the very popular Junior Ranger program. It's great!!

There are showers and laundry facilities in this area of the park.

The Grant Village area of the park has a campground and can handle a few smaller RVs but is mostly intended for tent camping or tent trailers. This is a popular campground during the busy summer season. Reservations can be made through Xanterra at 307-344-7311.

There is another campground in the vicinity of Grant Village. It's called Lewis Lake and is south of the Grant Village area. This is a smaller campground that is mostly intended for tent camping or pop-up tent trailers. It's also one of the last to fill up during the busy summer season. Reservations cannot be made, and this campground is a first-come first-serve campground. You have to be there to register for a campsite.

When you're done exploring the West Thumb and Grant Village areas of the park, head north again on the Lower Grand Loop Road back toward Fishing Bridge. Most times that's a right hand turn. You're going to be driving quite a ways as you'll go past both the Fishing Bridge area as well as the Canyon Village area. You'll continue heading straight across the main 4-way stop intersection at the Canyon Village area. You're now on the Upper Grand Loop Road. Keep going.

Mt. Washburn Hike:

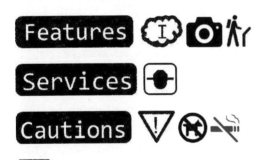

About five or six miles [about nine kilometers] up the road, you'll come to the Dunraven Pass summit. There is a parking lot on the right for the Mt. Washburn hike. This parking lot is under-sized and is full quite often during the busy summer season. Another parking area is at Chittenden Road, about four miles [about six kilometers] north of this parking area, right on the inside of a hairpin turn.

Mt. Washburn is one of the great hikes in Yellowstone National Park. You have a superb view from the top of the mountain, and if you have the physical ability to climb the mountain on a clear day you'll be richly rewarded with a southern view of Yellowstone National Park, which also includes the Grand Teton peaks in the distance, as well as being able to see the curvature of the earth. It's pretty spectacular. This location is also a park fire ranger lookout location. The building at the top is three stories with the top story looking like an airport control tower so the ranger has a 360 degree view of the park. After all, he's up there to watch for fires. The second floor is the residence area and the lower floor is for public viewing and is a great place for a picnic meal while enclosed in a glass room.

There are two ways to hike up to the top. From the Dunraven Pass parking lot, there is a trail that's about 6 miles [9.5 kilometers] roundtrip to the top of Mt. Washburn with stunning views on the way up. This trail is the more popular of the two. The second trail to the top of Mt. Washburn is from the next turnoff up the road to your right called Chittenden Road. Drive up Chittenden Road – a dirt road – to the top and park in the dirt parking lot. From the south end of the parking lot is the service road the park uses to get to the top of the mountain. This hike is a bit steeper than the Dunraven trail but it's only 4.2 miles [6.8 kilometers] long roundtrip. The difference in the two trails – setting aside that one is a service road – is that the trip up from the Chittenden Road side isn't as stunning as the Dunraven side because you're just hiking up a service road and most of the view is just going up the road. Maybe that's why the Dunraven trail is preferred by most. Take LOTS of pictures. (As a side note – if you're a bicyclist, you can bicycle up the service road from the Chittenden end to the top if you want to.)

The temperatures at the top of Mt. Washburn can be pretty cold. Brutally cold sometimes. It's also quite windy at the top, so when the cold temperatures and the wind combine, it can make the hike memorable for you for all the wrong reasons. Dress in layers and be ready for some very cold temperatures.

When you get back to your car in either parking lot, go to the entrance to that parking area, turn right, and continue to drive north on Upper Grand Loop Road.

Tower Fall Area:

Services ⊕ 🚻 🎁 ⛰ ⛱

Cautions ⚠ 🚫 🚭

🚗 As you drive up the road, you'll come into the Tower Fall area from the south. Park your vehicle in the main parking lot. Sometimes this can be a challenge, especially during the summer.

① 🌊 At this stop you'll want to walk out to the viewing platform for Tower Fall. It's about 100 yards [91 meters] or so from the parking area, and the trail is almost flat – just one little rise right in the middle. When you get out to the viewing platform, look to your right, and you'll see what's left of Grand Canyon of the Yellowstone. Look to your left and you'll see the waterfall. It's a ribbon style waterfall. Tower Fall is said to have many, many faces in the rock formations to the right and left of the waterfall and if you look hard enough, you'll see them. They are completely natural and are NOT man made. If you've been following the "waterfall plan", this ribbon style waterfall at Tower Fall is the last of the three waterfalls in the plan. Take pictures.

② As you walk back to the parking lot area, there is a gift shop located here. This is just

246

this ranger's opinion and take it if you want – it's totally up to you – but they have great ice cream in this gift shop.

In the Tower Fall area there is another first-come first-serve campground called Tower Fall Campground. This is a smaller campground that is mostly intended for tent camping or pop-up tent trailers. It's reasonably popular during the busy summer season. Reservations cannot be made and, again, this campground is a first-come first-serve campground. You have to be there to register for a campsite.

As you leave the Tower Fall area and drive north, you'll come across some Basalt rock columns near the side of the road (on your left). When Basalt rock cools, it forms giant columns that are six-sided and can be 40 to 50 feet [13 to 15 meters] tall or more. They look like huge crystals, only they're not, because they're not transparent – they're rock! They look really cool – no pun intended – and there are hundreds of them. As you enter this area, since they're along the side of the road, everyone will be able to see them, especially the driver. Now drivers ... don't get transfixed on them or there goes the paintjob on your car. Watch the road. Now everyone BUT the driver – look to the east (to your right) – and you'll see thousands more of these Basalt rock columns along the far side of the canyon wall of Grand Canyon of the Yellowstone. Take pictures.

Continue driving north out of the Basalt rock column area.

Tower-Roosevelt Area:

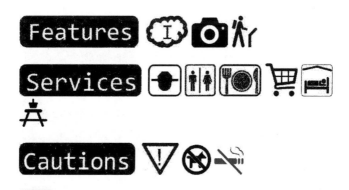

When driving into this area, you'll see a large intersection, and the Tower-Roosevelt complex will be off to your left. You'll see stables, corrals, a restaurant, cabins, and a whole array of other amenities. Turn left into this area.

This portion of the park is a road junction named for both the Tower area of the park together with the Roosevelt connection to the park. The Tower-Roosevelt junction connects the northern end of the park with the northeast entrance and Cooke City via the Lamar Valley and the north portion of the park at Mammoth Hot Springs.

(1) 📷 President Teddy Roosevelt did visit this area in the park in 1903 while he was here dedicating the entry arch at the north gate (more about that later). He stayed in the area but contrary to popular belief, he did NOT dine in the famous restaurant at Tower-Roosevelt junction as the lodge wasn't built until 1920. Keep in mind that back in 1903 the park was managed by the United States Army Cavalry stationed at Mammoth Hot Springs (more about that later too). Take pictures.

(2) This area is a good spot to take a break from the car and get out and walk around a bit.

(I) 🛏 This area also has rustic cabins and horse-drawn stagecoach rides as well as cowboy barbeques during the height of the summer visitation season. Reservations can be made through Xanterra at 307-344-7311.

🚗 When you're done at Tower-Roosevelt and back at the large intersection, drive straight across the intersection and head out toward Lamar Valley.

Lamar Valley Area:

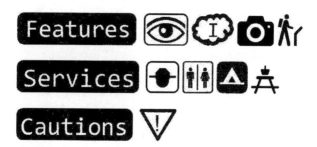

Features

Services

Cautions

The drive through Lamar Valley from the Tower-Roosevelt junction is remarkable. The road leads from the junction to Cooke City, and if you continue toward Red Lodge, you'll pass over the Bear Tooth Pass – a very curvy road with breathtaking views back toward the park. If you're traveling in an RV any larger than about 18 feet [5.5 meters], strongly consider what you might be facing. Most of the turns are tight hairpin turns, and the altitude is about 10,000 feet [3,048 meters] plus. Spring and fall temps are low, and spring drives are nice, but huge accumulations of snow during the winter and the carved-out road from the snowplows make the view back toward the park nearly impossible. This is also a major trouble area with black ice. This pass is closed any time it snows – even sometimes in the middle of summer. Take pictures if you can (be sure to stop safely off the roadway).

The Lamar Valley has lots of WILD animals. The primary animals that roam this area are bison, elk, pronghorn, wolves and an occasional grizzly bear. Seasonally, there are sometimes moose in the area as well. You'll probably get into animal jams (traffic jams caused by animals) as visitors try and take photos of wild animals. Most times the animals are a ways away and easy to photograph. Sometimes they are right up on the roadway, and people get way too close to them for their own safety. People DO get injured when attacked. Please stay a MINIMUM of 100 yards [91 meters] away from bears and wolves, and 25 yards [23 meters] away from ALL OTHER wild animals. Drive safely, keep your distance from animals, and take pictures.

①📷 As you're heading eastward from the Tower-Roosevelt junction, you'll pass through an area with large boulders on the left edge of the road and just about the time when you get a first glimpse of the Lamar River, you'll be at the top of a small hill. There are turnouts to your right, and if you stop during the warmer months there is a nesting pair of Osprey just across the river high up in the trees. They seem to be there every season. There are also nesting pairs of Eagles as well, but not seen as often as the Osprey. Take pictures.

②📷 As you continue traveling down the small hill you'll see a small sign on the right edge of the road marking the beginning of the Lamar Valley. The valley is home to several herds of bison and elk, and seasonally moose visit this area of the park. Pronghorn antelope and wolves are present, as well as an occasional grizzly bear. Lots of other smaller animals inhabit the valley too. Take pictures.

③ 📷 As you travel out through the valley, on your left (north side of the road) is Buffalo Ranch. This is where the bison of Yellowstone National Park were revived after they were almost wiped out in the early 1900s. This area is now a conservation post and an area where the Yellowstone conference center is. There are also classes on all sorts of nature driven programs. Check the course descriptions and take a class, if you have the time. Information is in the park newsletter. Take pictures if you like.

④ 📷 As you enter the furthest part of the Lamar Valley road nearing the towns of Silver Gate and Cooke City, look to your left up on top of the cliff areas for Big Horn Sheep. This is one of the areas they tend to frequent. You'll probably need binoculars and a good telephoto lens on your camera, but they're up there. Take pictures.

ⓘ 🚻 There are no services at all in the Lamar Valley area other than gravity style restroom facilities at the road leading to Slough Creek Campground and a couple more in one of the larger turnouts toward the northeast gate on the south side of the road.

🗨️⚠️ Within the Lamar Valley there are two campgrounds. The first is Slough Creek Campground located midway in the valley. The second is Pebble Creek Campground located further to the east toward the north-eastern gate to the park. Both are reasonably popular during the busy summer season with fishing activities. Reservations cannot be made, and these two campgrounds are both on a first-come first-serve basis. You have to be there to register for a campsite.

🚗 Drive out of the Lamar Valley the way you came in. Turn right again at that large Tower-Roosevelt intersection you saw earlier. You'll be heading west on the Upper Grand Loop Road.

Petrified Tree:

Features 🗨️ 📷 🚶

🚗 Petrified Tree entrance road will be on your left after you leave the Tower-Roosevelt junction. Turn left into this area.

(1) 📷 The road is all of a quarter-mile long and dead ends at the Petrified Tree. Walk up the slight incline to the tree. Please respect the fence. Take pictures.

💭 This area has been frequented by moose, especially early or late in the summer season. Watch the hill areas to the south of the Petrified Tree road for these animals. Take pictures.

🚗 When you drive out of the Petrified Tree area, turn left at the intersection with the Upper Grand Loop Road and continue to head toward Mammoth Hot Springs.

Wraith Falls and Undine Falls (hikes):

Features 🌊📷🚶

🚗 Both of these waterfalls are a few miles from and to the east of the Mammoth Hot Springs area. Wraith Falls will be on your left, and you'll come to it first. Park in the lot on your left. Undine Falls is just up the road a bit on the right, and you can park in that lot as well.

① 🌊🚶 These two waterfalls have very nice and somewhat easy hikes up to each waterfall. The trailheads are right along the edge of the roadway with Wraith being on the south side of the road and Undine on the north side. Take pictures.

🚗 Continue driving toward Mammoth Hot Springs (to the west).

Mammoth Hot Springs:

🚗 As you enter the Mammoth Hot Springs area you'll come to an intersection. Turn left and drive towards the parking areas and park your car along the right side of the hill. RV parking at the bottom of the hill below the terraces is very limited, even for smaller RVs. The park has set aside the east side (on your left) of the road for larger vehicles, but most times cars have invaded that area too. Do the best you can when parking your RV but be ready for someone to block you in and make it a challenge to get out of there.

Located in this part of the park is Mammoth Hot Springs, a large concentration of layered terraces of super-heated water. The water contains high concentrations of Travertine in solution which, when the water crests over the edge of each pool, drops microscopic amounts of Travertine minerals at the top edge of the pool which form the pools.

There is a National Park Service Albright Visitor Center in this part of the park. During the summer visitation season there are National Park Service rangers who can help guide you to anywhere in the park you'd like to go. Just stop in and ask.

The National Park Service Visitor Center in the Mammoth area is called the Albright Visitor Center, and its main focus is all about the history of Yellowstone National Park. Take pictures.

The Mammoth area of the park is Yellowstone National Park headquarters. You'll notice a larger presence of government vehicles in this area as well as quite an array of visitor amenities.

1 The terraces are best viewed from the lower area but that can change from season to season. Look for steam wafting up and that's your clue on which way to go. Walk

up onto one of the boardwalks in this area, and you'll see the terraces right in front of you. Stay on the boardwalks, please. Serious damage can be done to the fragile terrace framework if you leave the boardwalks for any reason. Since the best viewing areas for the terraces change from year to year so it's always wise to ask at the National Park Service Visitor Center for the latest information. Take pictures.

Driving northward out of the main area of Mammoth Hot Springs toward the north entrance gate brings you down a short hill to the campground area. Continuing further down another hill and a curvy road will bring you past cliffs.

②📷 This area is visited by Big Horn Sheep. You don't need binoculars here. They're easy to see, when they're there. Take pictures.

Continuing further down the hill will bring you to the north entrance station. Go ahead and exit this station and drive out to the area by the Roosevelt Arch. You can see it from the north entrance gate.

③📷 This is the archway that was dedicated back in 1903 by President Theodore Roosevelt as the main entrance to the park. Notice how narrow the opening is. It was built for the largest vehicles of the time – Model A

Ford's – and is a bit narrow for today's modern vehicles. If you want to take pictures of the Roosevelt Arch (I can't blame you), the best thing to do is to park across the street from some of the shops in Gardiner, and walk back. The Roosevelt Arch is beautiful and historic. Take pictures.

④ If you have the time, the town of Gardiner is a quaint little town that has restaurants, gas stations, hotels, gift shops and more. This little town used to be the railroad stopping point for visitors to the park as late as the middle of the last century.

Drive back through the north entrance gate and up to the Mammoth Hot Springs area. Continue to drive south past the main part of the Mammoth area and up the hill at the south end. If you have a standard sized automobile or small truck, you can drive along the Upper Terrace Drive just south of the terraces. At the top of the hill, there's an entrance (on your right) to the Upper Terrace Loop.

DO NOT go into this drive if you're towing anything, in a bus of any sort, in an RV of any length, have a dually, or are larger than a normal vehicle. You'll see a 'restriction' sign at the entrance so if you're in a larger vehicle, park just outside the gate with all the tour buses, as the road is very narrow in spots and you WILL just get stuck – the tow bills, we've heard, are pretty stiff for a tow truck to get you out. Please don't drive in there in any vehicle larger than a normal one.

(5) ♨ You can walk on the boardwalks and get into this area from the Lower Terrace boardwalk loops as well. In a normal vehicle, you can enter the gate, stay to the right and park about a hundred yards [91 meters] or so into the drive. Walk down into an older area of Mammoth Hot Springs and see what happens after eons of Travertine minerals continually depositing themselves. The area looks somewhat like the moon. Take pictures.

(I) 📷 In the fall, during the elk rut, there are usually large concentrations of elk walking about in the Mammoth Hot Springs area. Remember I mentioned to stay a minimum of 25 yards [23 meters] away from these animals. They are capable of charging you or standing on their hind legs – much like a dog would do – and swinging their front feet at you in a bicycle type motion. The hooves on the end of those two front feet are very hard and can tear you up. If there are males present – the ones with the antlers – they are very protective of their harems of females. STAY AT LEAST 25 YARDS [23 METERS] AWAY FROM ALL ANIMALS, including the elk. Park service rangers are usually around to keep people at a safe distance. Please don't get too close as we want you to leave the park with your health intact. Thanks.

There is an amphitheater near the campground in this area of the park. There are nightly ranger-led power point presentations about historical, natural, hydrothermal, cultural, or animal related topics in the park. The programs begin at dusk and start times vary with the season, so check at one of the visitor centers for the times. You can also check for the times in the green section in the middle of the park newspaper available when you entered the park, or you can pick one up at a visitor center.

This area is one of nine locations in the park that operate the Junior Ranger Program. There is a National Park Service Visitor Center in this area where you can purchase the Junior Ranger materials for a nominal fee. A ranger can explain how the program works to your child/children. Age range is from 4 years to 13+ years of age, but it's actually fun for the whole family. So don't let age stop you from participating in the very popular Junior Ranger program. It's great!!

Located in the Mammoth Hot Springs area is the Mammoth Hot Springs Hotel. It's one of the famous old historic structures in the park. If you're looking for historic and upscale, this is the place. Located in the heart of the Mammoth area you can walk to virtually everything worth seeing in the area. This is a very popular place to stay in the park and reservations are a must during the busy season. Reservations can be made through Xanterra at 307-344-7311.

 In the vicinity of the Mammoth Hot Springs area there is a campground. It's located down the first hill from the main Mammoth Hot Springs area. This is a reasonably popular campground during the summer season. Reservations cannot be made as this campground is on a first-come first-serve basis only. You have to be there to register for a campsite.

As you leave the Upper Terraces area, you'll want to go south. For most normal sized vehicles this is a right turn. If you parked out by the tour buses, because you are in a larger than normal vehicle, just head south away from the main Mammoth Hot Springs area.

Sheepeater Cliff:

Features

Services

Cautions

Driving south out of the Mammoth Hot Springs area, you'll come to the Sheepeater Cliff picnic area. Turn left into this area.

Please do NOT drive your RV, even if it is a smaller RV, into this area as you'll have great difficulty getting turned around in the very small parking lot. This is a prohibited area for RVs and law enforcement rangers check the area frequently.

The Sheepeater Cliff area is all part of a series of huge Basalt rock flows that occurred in the Tower Fall area and extending all the way over to the Tower Fall area sixteen miles [26 kilometers] to the east. If you remember, the Basalt rock over near Tower Fall was tan colored, while this Basalt rock is dark gray. Same rock ... different color. Take pictures.

Just south of Sheepeater Cliff area there is a campground. It's called Indian Creek. This is a reasonably popular campground during the summer season. Reservations cannot be made as this campground is on a first-come first-serve

basis only. You have to be there to register for
a campsite.

 Turn left on Upper Grand Loop Road and head
south.

Norris Geyser Basin Area:

 As you're heading south on the Upper Grand
Loop Road, you'll come to the Norris Geyser Basin
area.

Just north of the main intersection at Norris
Geyser Basin (to your left) is the Museum of the
National Park Ranger. This little building is one of the
original buildings built during the time when the U.S.
Army Cavalry occupied the park and serves today as a
museum to educate the public about the origins of the
National Park Service and the ranger corp. There are
all sorts of artifacts related to rangers in the park,
information about the history of the park service,
about the transition from the U.S. Army Cavalry to

the National Park Service, etc. It's a pretty interesting place, if you have the time. Take pictures.

Now drive south a very short distance back on the Upper Grand Loop Road. You'll come across that same large 4-way stop intersection at Norris Geyser Basin area that we were at earlier in this plan. Remember this intersection? Turn right into Norris Geyser Basin.

There is a National Park Service Museum and Information Station in this part of the park. During the summer visitation season there are National Park Service rangers who can help guide you to anywhere in the park you'd like to go. Just stop in and ask.

This area is also very popular in the summer season and the parking lot becomes overloaded quite easily. If you see a road barrier up near the entrance to Norris Geyser Basin, this means law enforcement rangers are metering cars into and out of the parking lot to avoid gridlock. Just wait a short while out by the main intersection, and they'll let you in based on the number of cars exiting the area.

1 Norris Geyser Basin. This is the oldest, most dramatic, and geologically active area of the park. This geyser basin is home to the world's tallest geyser – Steamboat Geyser – that erupts on a very sporadic basis. When it does go off, it's something to behold. After the initial eruptive event which lasts only

a short time, the geyser goes into a steam phase with steam blasting up about 300 feet [91 meters] for about 24 hours. There's also a walkway that goes right over a geo-thermal area, as well as loads of other geysers, hot springs, and steam vents. Take pictures.

This area is one of nine locations in the park that operate the Junior Ranger Program. There is a National Park Service Information Station in this area where you can purchase the Junior Ranger materials for a nominal fee. A ranger can explain how the program works to your child/children. Age range is from 4 years to 13+ years of age, but it's actually fun for the whole family. So don't let age stop you from participating in the very popular Junior Ranger program. It's great!!

Near the Norris Geyser Basin is the Norris Campground. It's located just north of the main junction entrance to the geyser basin. This is a reasonably popular campground during the summer season. Reservations cannot be made as this campground is on a first-come first-serve basis only. You have to be there to register for a campsite.

This is the end of this Five+ Day Ranger Plan. I hope you had a good time, enjoyed the park, and are excited about coming back again soon. Thank you for following this plan.

Please drive safely as you leave the park.

NOTE FROM THE AUTHOR

Please do me a huge favor. IF you like this book and it helped you navigate your way around Yellowstone, please, please, please ... take a moment and let the world know through social media such as Facebook, Twitter, email and text messaging, and please write a review. Thank you.

Chapter Ten

My Last Thoughts

You know, I've met people from all over the world who come to visit Yellowstone National Park. They come in all shapes, sizes, ages, and backgrounds. Most I can communicate with just fine; a few are challenges mostly because of a language barrier. Some are challenges for other reasons.

There are also visitors that come to the park completely unprepared for the crowds. They get up to the desk and ask me what they can see in two days. And by the way, we need a campground space and don't have a reservation. They actually expect to come to a place that regularly has four million plus visitors yet is designed for two million – so everything is two hundred percent overloaded – and expect to get ahead of all the others who made reservations or are already in the park. Where do these expectations come from? Seeing the entire park is completely out of the range of possibility as they only allowed themselves two days. They're very disappointed they have to pick and choose which things in the park they just can't make it to. They're surprised the campgrounds are fully booked up, and the hotels in the towns surrounding the park are booked too. What sometimes happens at the visitors desk is they overhear me telling a couple in front of them in line that also only have two days in the park they'll have to pick and choose, then when it's time for the hurried couple to step up to the desk, they tell me they have four days in the park (instead of the two days they actually have) so I'll show them more things. They're now forced to scurry around the park like a bat out of heck – traveling in excess of every speed limit they come across – parking their full-sized SUV in parking spaces that are way too tiny for a vehicle that size or not parking legally at all, tick a bunch of other people off, then try and blame their poor visit on the rangers somehow. Most times we can't help them too much – about the park AND about life. And it's sad for so many reasons.

Every ranger in the park is trying their utmost to give every visitor to the park the best experience we can while helping them return home safely in one piece. It doesn't matter where this visitor came from. Yet every year people are injured or killed because they do something that is not only unlawful, but downright dangerous as well. Some DO pay the ultimate price. And that's very sad for all of us that try so hard to keep it from happening. Maybe somehow this book might inspire just one extra person that may have thoughts about doing something stupid, like getting too close to an animal or a hydro-thermal feature, to listen to what we try and tell them and stay a safe distance away. Or, maybe, this book might inspire people to take the time to actually plan their visit and allow enough time to see what they want to see – you know, four or five days. If this book doesn't do anything more than that, then all the effort that went into this book will make it all worthwhile, for this ranger anyway.

As rangers, we also try VERY hard to please each visitor we come in contact with hoping they can have a great time in Yellowstone National Park. We work tirelessly trying to merge the number of days the visitor sets aside to see the park, with where they're staying, with what they're trying to see and experience into a plan that works for them. But we're also not magicians. We're rangers in one of the best national parks in the country. A park about thirty five hundred square miles [9,065 square kilometers] in size that takes about three plus hours to go from one side to the other.

So if you're trying to visit a place where there are ten thousand hydro-thermal and geo-thermal features, almost three hundred waterfalls, over four hundred grizzly bears, about six hundred plus black bears, over five thousand bison, approximately seventy five hundred elk, and about one hundred wolves – not to mention loads of other critters of all shapes and sizes – miles and miles of rivers, and about a thousand miles of trails to hike, then come visit Yellowstone National Park. Come with hotel, lodging or campground reservations. Come with some sort of plan on what you want to see. And come with your eyes wide open, and we'll show you a place where we'll open those eyes even further. We WILL be glad to see you walk up to the visitor's center desk and ask a question.

I hope we see you soon!

ACKNOWLEDGMENTS

I'd like to take this opportunity to personally thank each of the people who helped me with this endeavor. First, and most importantly, I'd like to thank Robert D. Bovenschulte for the tremendous help he was in editing this book. I'm a ranger in the park and not an editor. With Bob's expertise and editing skills that go WAY beyond any I could ever hope to learn, he did a fantastic job in editing this book. Thanks, Bob.

I'd also like to single out a few other people who helped me along the way. I had some help from my family, namely Kevin Nullmeyer, our son, and our daughter, Carrie Greco. They helped me single out a few areas that needed fine-tuning here and there. Thanks, kids. I love you.

I also received some help with concepts and content from a very good friend of mine, David Araki. Dave has always been an inspiration in my life to give me guidance when I sometimes stray off course and he and I have known each other for thirty plus years. He knows just what to say to me, at just the right time, and I value having him in my life. Thanks, Dave.

I'd also like to thank a good friend and fellow ranger, Doug Kehl, for helping with portions of the book. He's one of those guys that everyone likes and he's helped me in so many ways. He is a great friend.

I also appreciate the editing support provided by Linda Russell, a close friend of mine. She was very helpful in providing some editing assistance and guidance. Thank you, Linda.

And no author worth his weight would ever forget the help of their spouse. My wife, Jan, has always been there for me even when I made some very big mistakes. She is my rock and the love of my life. I'm glad when she tells me, "You can't say that!" or "You should think that out more as it sounds like (whatever)." And you know what? She's always right. Thank you, honey.

And last, but certainly not least, I'd be remiss if I didn't thank all the people who have visited Yellowstone National Park. They're the ones that walked up to the visitor center desk and asked all those questions about the park that inspired me to write this book to offer people some self-guidance.

Thank you ALL.

ABOUT THE AUTHOR

R.D. Nullmeyer has been a seasonal ranger in Yellowstone National Park for multiple seasons and has first-hand experience with the huge number of visitors that Yellowstone draws each season. His duties include answering questions from visitors from all over the world to Yellowstone Park, giving short talks regarding wildlife safety and exploring Yellowstone, afternoon talks about park related subjects, as well as evening campfire talks to large groups of people. He also gives small talks to kids in the Junior Ranger Program. He loves the "second part" of his life.

Besides his ranger endeavors, he is a retired successful real estate broker, he is also a licensed pilot, holds a United States patent, and has written extensive training manuals for professional courses.

In these achievements, he has perfected the unique ability to straighten out people's perspectives of national parks and make their visit more enjoyable, while maintaining some level of visitor safety along the way. His goal with every visitor is for them to have the best time they've ever had.

This is precisely why he put this book together. That is, to help visitors to Yellowstone have the best time they could possibly have with whatever time they have to devote to their visit.

Spend a few minutes and read about how you can

self-plan your own visit to Yellowstone National Park by following his Ranger Day Plans. Whether you only have one day or a week, there's a Ranger Day Plan that will fulfill your expectation of seeing things you never knew existed.

Yellowstone National Park is quite a place.

83535512R00162

Made in the USA
San Bernardino, CA
27 July 2018